HOLT SCIENCE & TECHNOLOGY

Water on Earth

HOLT, RINEHART AND WINSTON

A Harcourt Classroom Education Company

Austin · New York · Orlando · Atlanta · San Francisco · Boston · Dallas · Toronto · London

Staff Credits

Editorial

Robert W. Todd, Executive Editor

Robert V. Tucek, Leigh Ann Garcia, Senior Editors

Clay Walton, Jim Ratcliffe, Editors

ANCILLARIES

Jennifer Childers, Senior Editor

Chris Colby, Molly Frohlich, Shari Husain, Kristen McCardel, Sabelyn Pussman, Erin Roberson

COPYEDITING

Dawn Spinozza, Copyediting Supervisor

EDITORIAL SUPPORT STAFF

Jeanne Graham, Mary Helbling, Tanu'e White, Doug Rutley

EDITORIAL PERMISSIONS

Cathy Paré, Permissions Manager

Jan Harrington, Permissions Editor

Art, Design, and Photo

BOOK DESIGN

Richard Metzger, Design Director

Marc Cooper, Senior Designer

José Garza, Designer

Alicia Sullivan, Designer (ATE), Cristina Bowerman, Design Associate (ATE), Eric Rupprath, Designer (Ancillaries), Holly Whittaker, Traffic Coordinator

IMAGE ACQUISITIONS

Joe London, Director

Elaine Tate, Art Buyer Supervisor

Jeannie Taylor, Photo Research Supervisor

Andy Christiansen, Photo Researcher

Jackie Berger, Assistant Photo Researcher

PHOTO STUDIO

Sam Dudgeon, Senior Staff Photographer

Victoria Smith, Photo Specialist

Lauren Eischen, Photo Coordinator

DESIGN NEW MEDIA

Susan Michael, Design Director

Production

Mimi Stockdell, Senior Production Manager

Beth Sample, Senior Production Coordinator

Suzanne Brooks, Sara Carroll-Downs

Media Production

Kim A. Scott, Senior Production Manager

Adriana Bardin-Prestwood, Senior Production Coordinator

New Media

Armin Gutzmer, Director

Jim Bruno, Senior Project Manager

Lydia Doty, Senior Project Manager

Jessica Bega, Project Manager

Cathy Kuhles, Nina Degollado, Technical Assistants

Design Implementation and Production

The Quarasan Group, Inc.

Acknowledgments

Chapter Writers

Kathleen Meehan Berry
Science Chairman
Canon-McMillan School
  District
Canonsburg, Pennsylvania

Robert H. Fronk, Ph.D.
*Chair of Science and
  Mathematics Education
  Department*
Florida Institute of Technology
West Melbourne, Florida

**Mary Kay Hemenway,
Ph.D.**
*Research Associate and Senior
  Lecturer*
Department of Astronomy
The University of Texas
Austin, Texas

Kathleen Kaska
Life and Earth Science Teacher
Lake Travis Middle School
Austin, Texas

Peter E. Malin, Ph.D.
Professor of Geology
Division of Earth and Ocean
  Sciences
Duke University
Durham, North Carolina

Karen J. Meech, Ph.D.
Associate Astronomer
Institute for Astronomy
University of Hawaii
Honolulu, Hawaii

Robert J. Sager
*Chair and Professor of Earth
  Sciences*
Pierce College
Lakewood, Washington

Lab Writers

Kenneth Creese
Science Teacher
White Mountain Junior
  High School
Rock Springs, Wyoming

Linda A. Culp
Science Teacher and Dept. Chair
Thorndale High School
Thorndale, Texas

Bruce M. Jones
Science Teacher and Dept. Chair
The Blake School
Minneapolis, Minnesota

Shannon Miller
Science and Math Teacher
Llano Junior High School
Llano, Texas

Robert Stephen Ricks
Special Services Teacher
Department of Classroom
  Improvement
Alabama State Department
  of Education
Montgomery, Alabama

James J. Secosky
Science Teacher
Bloomfield Central School
Bloomfield, New York

Academic Reviewers

Mead Allison, Ph.D.
*Assistant Professor of
  Oceanography*
Texas A&M University
Galveston, Texas

Alissa Arp, Ph.D.
*Director and Professor of
  Environmental Studies*
Romberg Tiburon Center
San Francisco State University
Tiburon, California

Paul D. Asimow, Ph.D.
*Assistant Professor of Geology
  and Geochemistry*
Department of Physics and
  Planetary Sciences
California Institute of
  Technology
Pasadena, California

G. Fritz Benedict, Ph.D.
*Senior Research Scientist and
  Astronomer*
McDonald Observatory
The University of Texas
Austin, Texas

**Russell M. Brengelman,
Ph.D.**
Professor of Physics
Morehead State University
Morehead, Kentucky

John A. Brockhaus, Ph.D.
*Director—Mapping, Charting,
  and Geodesy Program*
Department of Geography and
  Environmental Engineering
United States Military Academy
West Point, New York

Michael Brown, Ph.D.
*Assistant Professor of Planetary
  Astronomy*
Department of Physics
  and Astronomy
California Institute of
  Technology
Pasadena, California

Wesley N. Colley, Ph.D.
Postdoctoral Fellow
Harvard-Smithsonian Center
  for Astrophysics
Cambridge, Massachusetts

Andrew J. Davis, Ph.D.
*Manager—ACE Science Data
  Center*
Physics Department
California Institute of
  Technology
Pasadena, California

Peter E. Demmin, Ed.D.
*Former Science Teacher and
  Department Chair*
Amherst Central High School
Amherst, New York

James Denbow, Ph.D.
Associate Professor
Department of Anthropology
The University of Texas
Austin, Texas

Roy W. Hann, Jr., Ph.D.
Professor of Civil Engineering
Texas A&M University
College Station, Texas

Frederick R. Heck, Ph.D.
Professor of Geology
Ferris State University
Big Rapids, Michigan

Richard Hey, Ph.D.
Professor of Geophysics
Hawaii Institute of Geophysics
  and Planetology
University of Hawaii
Honolulu, Hawaii

John E. Hoover, Ph.D.
Associate Professor of Biology
Millersville University
Millersville, Pennsylvania

**Robert W. Houghton,
Ph.D.**
Senior Staff Associate
Lamont-Doherty Earth
  Observatory
Columbia University
Palisades, New York

Steven A. Jennings, Ph.D.
Assistant Professor
Department of Geography &
  Environmental Studies
University of Colorado
Colorado Springs, Colorado

Eric L. Johnson, Ph.D.
Assistant Professor of Geology
Central Michigan University
Mount Pleasant, Michigan

John Kermond, Ph.D.
Visiting Scientist
NOAA–Office of Global
  Programs
Silver Spring, Maryland

Zavareh Kothavala, Ph.D.
Postdoctoral Associate Scientist
Department of Geology and
  Geophysics
Yale University
New Haven, Connecticut

Karen Kwitter, Ph.D.
*Ebenezer Fitch Professor of
  Astronomy*
Williams College
Williamstown, Massachusetts

Valerie Lang, Ph.D.
*Project Leader of Environmental
  Programs*
The Aerospace Corporation
Los Angeles, California

Philip LaRoe
Professor
Helena College of Technology
Helena, Montana

Julie Lutz, Ph.D.
Astronomy Program
Washington State University
Pullman, Washington

Duane F. Marble, Ph.D.
Professor Emeritus
Department of Geography and
  Natural Resources
Ohio State University
Columbus, Ohio

Joseph A. McClure, Ph.D.
Associate Professor
Department of Physics
Georgetown University
Washington, D.C.

Frank K. McKinney, Ph.D.
Professor of Geology
Appalachian State University
Boone, North Carolina

Joann Mossa, Ph.D.
Associate Professor of Geography
University of Florida
Gainesville, Florida

LaMoine L. Motz, Ph.D.
Coordinator of Science Education
Department of Learning
  Services
Oakland County Schools
Waterford, Michigan

Barbara Murck, Ph.D.
*Assistant Professor of Earth
  Science*
Erindale College
University of Toronto
Mississauga, Ontario
CANADA

**Hilary Clement Olson,
Ph.D.**
Research Associate
Institute for Geophysics
The University of Texas
Austin, Texas

Andre Potochnik
Geologist
Grand Canyon Field Institute
Flagstaff, Arizona

John R. Reid, Ph.D.
Professor Emeritus
Department of Geology and
  Geological Engineering
University of North Dakota
Grand Forks, North Dakota

Gary Rottman, Ph.D.
Associate Director
Laboratory for Atmosphere
  and Space Physics
University of Colorado
Boulder, Colorado

Dork L. Sahagian, Ph.D.
Professor
Institute for the Study of
  Earth, Oceans, and Space
University of New Hampshire
Durham, New Hampshire

Peter Sheridan, Ph.D.
Professor of Chemistry
Colgate University
Hamilton, New York

David Sprayberry, Ph.D.
*Assistant Director for Observing
  Support*
W.M. Keck Observatory
California Association for
  Research in Astronomy
Kamuela, Hawaii

Lynne Talley, Ph.D.
Professor
Scripps Institution of
  Oceanography
University of California
La Jolla, California

Acknowledgments (cont.)

Glenn Thompson, Ph.D.
Scientist
Geophysical Institute
University of Alaska
Fairbanks, Alaska

Martin VanDyke, Ph.D.
Professor of Chemistry, Emeritus
Front Range Community
College
Westminister, Colorado

Thad A. Wasklewicz, Ph.D.
Assistant Professor of Geography
University of Memphis
Memphis, Tennessee

Hans Rudolf Wenk, Ph.D.
Professor of Geology and Geophysical Sciences
University of California
Berkeley, California

Lisa D. White, Ph.D.
Associate Professor of Geosciences
San Francisco State University
San Francisco, California

Lorraine W. Wolf, Ph.D.
Associate Professor of Geology
Auburn University
Auburn, Alabama

Charles A. Wood, Ph.D.
Chairman and Professor of Space Studies
University of North Dakota
Grand Forks, North Dakota

Safety Reviewer

Jack Gerlovich, Ph.D.
Associate Professor
School of Education
Drake University
Des Moines, Iowa

Teacher Reviewers

Barry L. Bishop
Science Teacher and Dept. Chair
San Rafael Junior High School
Ferron, Utah

Yvonne Brannum
Science Teacher and Dept. Chair
Hine Junior High School
Washington, D.C.

Daniel L. Bugenhagen
Science Teacher and Dept. Chair
Yutan Junior & Senior High
School
Yutan, Nebraska

Kenneth Creese
Science Teacher
White Mountain Junior High
School
Rock Springs, Wyoming

Linda A. Culp
Science Teacher and Dept. Chair
Thorndale High School
Thorndale, Texas

Alonda Droege
Science Teacher
Pioneer Middle School
Steilacom, Washington

Laura Fleet
Science Teacher
Alice B. Landrum Middle
School
Ponte Vedra Beach, Florida

Susan Gorman
Science Teacher
Northridge Middle School
North Richland Hills, Texas

C. John Graves
Science Teacher
Monforton Middle School
Bozeman, Montana

Janel Guse
Science Teacher and Dept. Chair
West Central Middle School
Hartford, South Dakota

Gary Habeeb
Science Mentor
Sierra–Plumas Joint Unified
School District
Downieville, California

Dennis Hanson
Science Teacher and Dept. Chair
Big Bear Middle School
Big Bear Lake, California

Norman E. Holcomb
Science Teacher
Marion Local Schools
Maria Stein, Ohio

Tracy Jahn
Science Teacher
Berkshire Junior-Senior High
School
Canaan, New York

David D. Jones
Science Teacher
Andrew Jackson Middle School
Cross Lanes, West Virginia

Howard A. Knodle
Science Teacher
Belvidere High School
Belvidere, Illinois

Michael E. Kral
Science Teacher
West Hardin Middle School
Cecilia, Kentucky

Kathy LaRoe
Science Teacher
East Valley Middle School
East Helena, Montana

Scott Mandel, Ph.D.
Director and Educational Consultant
Teachers Helping Teachers
Los Angeles, California

Kathy McKee
Science Teacher
Hoyt Middle School
Des Moines, Iowa

Michael Minium
Vice President of Program Development
United States Orienteering
Federation
Forest Park, Georgia

Jan Nelson
Science Teacher
East Valley Middle School
East Helena, Montana

Dwight C. Patton
Science Teacher
Carroll T. Welch Middle
School
Horizon City, Texas

Joseph Price
Chairman—Science Department
H. M. Brown Junior High
School
Washington, D.C.

Terry J. Rakes
Science Teacher
Elmwood Junior High School
Rogers, Arkansas

Steven Ramig
Science Teacher
West Point High School
West Point, Nebraska

Helen P. Schiller
Science Teacher
Northwood Middle School
Taylors, South Carolina

Bert J. Sherwood
Science Teacher
Socorro Middle School
El Paso, Texas

Larry Tackett
Science Teacher and Dept. Chair
Andrew Jackson Middle School
Cross Lanes, West Virginia

Walter Woolbaugh
Science Teacher
Manhattan Junior High School
Manhattan, Montana

Alexis S. Wright
Middle School Science Coordinator
Rye Country Day School
Rye, New York

Gordon Zibelman
Science Teacher
Drexel Hill Middle School
Drexel Hill, Pennsylvania

Water on Earth

Skills Development

To the Student

This book was created to make your science experience interesting, exciting, and fun!

Go for It!

Science is a process of discovery, a trek into the unknown. The skills you develop using *Holt Science & Technology*— such as observing, experimenting, and explaining observations and ideas— are the skills you will need for the future. There is a universe of exploration and discovery awaiting those who accept the challenges of science.

Science & Technology

You see the interaction between science and technology every day. Science makes technology possible. On the other hand, some of the products of technology, such as computers, are used to make further scientific discoveries. In fact, much of the scientific work that is done today has become so technically complicated and expensive that no one person can do it entirely alone. But make no mistake, the creative ideas for even the most highly technical and expensive scientific work still come from individuals.

Activities and Labs

The activities and labs in this book will allow you to make some basic but important scientific discoveries on your own. You can even do some exploring on your own at home! Here's your chance to use your imagination and curiosity as you investigate your world.

Keep a ScienceLog

In this book, you will be asked to keep a type of journal called a ScienceLog to record your thoughts, observations, experiments, and conclusions. As you develop your ScienceLog, you will see your own ideas taking shape over time. You'll have a written record of how your ideas have changed as you learn about and explore interesting topics in science.

Know "What You'll Do"

The "What You'll Do" list at the beginning of each section is your built-in guide to what you need to learn in each chapter. When you can answer the questions in the Section Review and Chapter Review, you know you are ready for a test.

Check Out the Internet

You will see this *sciLINKS* logo throughout the book. You'll be using *sci*LINKS as your gateway to the Internet. Once you log on to *sci*LINKS using your computer's Internet link, type in the *sci*LINKS address. When asked for the keyword code, type in the keyword for that topic. A wealth of resources is now at your disposal to help you learn more about that topic.

In addition to *sci*LINKS you can log on to some other great resources to go with your text. The addresses shown below will take you to the home page of each site.

This textbook contains the following on-line resources to help you make the most of your science experience.

 go. hrw .com

Visit **go.hrw.com** for extra help and study aids matched to your textbook. Just type in the keyword HST HOME.

*sci*LINKS. NSTA

Visit **www.scilinks.org** to find resources specific to topics in your textbook. Keywords appear throughout your book to take you further.

Smithsonian Institution®
Internet Connections

Visit **www.si.edu/hrw** for specifically chosen on-line materials from one of our nation's premier science museums.

CNNfyi.com

Visit **www.cnnfyi.com** for late-breaking news and current events stories selected just for you.

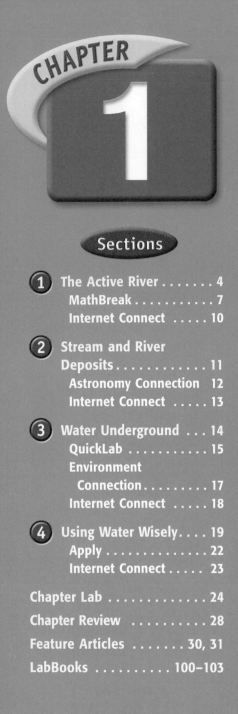

CHAPTER 1

Sections

Pre-Reading
Questions

1. What role does water play in shaping the surface of the Earth?
2. What is the difference between erosion and deposition?

The Flow of Fresh Water

THE SOUND IS DEAFENING

You can hear the thundering roar of Iguaçu (EE gwah SOO) Falls for miles. The Iguaçu River travels more than 500 km across Brazil before it tumbles off the edge of a volcanic plateau in a series of 275 individual waterfalls separated by forested islands. Over the past 20,000 years, erosion has caused the falls to move 28 km upstream. Where will they be 20,000 years from now? In this chapter, you will learn how flowing water shapes Earth's surface.

STREAM WEAVERS

How do streams and river systems develop? Do the following activity to find out.

Procedure

1. Begin with a **bucket of sand** and enough **gravel** to fill the bottom of a **rectangular plastic washtub.**

2. Spread the gravel in a layer at the bottom of the washtub. Place 4–6 cm of sand on top of the gravel. Add more sand to one end of the washtub to form a slope.

3. Make a small hole in the bottom of a **paper cup.** Attach the cup to the inside of the tub with a **clothespin.** The cup should be placed at the end that has more sand. Fill the cup with water, and observe the **water** as it moves over the sand. Use a **magnifying lens** to observe features of the stream more closely.

4. Record your observations in your ScienceLog.

Analysis

5. At the start of your experiment, how did the moving water affect the sand?

6. As time passed, how did the moving water affect the sand?

7. Explain how this activity modeled the development of streams. In what ways was it accurate? How was it inaccurate?

The Flow of Fresh Water   3

Terms to Learn

erosion   divide
water cycle   channel
tributary   load
drainage basin

What You'll Do

◆ Illustrate the water cycle.
◆ Describe a drainage basin.
◆ Explain the major factors that affect the rate of stream erosion.
◆ Identify the stages of river development.

The Active River

You are probably familiar with the Grand Canyon, shown in **Figure 1.** But did you know that about 6 million years ago, the area now known as the Grand Canyon was nearly as flat as a pancake? The Colorado River cut down into the rock and formed the Grand Canyon over millions of years by washing billions of tons of soil and rock from its riverbed. This process is a type of *erosion*. **Erosion** is the removal and transport of surface material, such as rock and soil. Rivers are not the only agents of erosion. Wind, rain, ice, and snow can cause erosion as well.

Because of erosion caused by water, the Grand Canyon is now about 1.6 km deep and 446 km long. In this section, you will learn about stream development, river systems, and the different factors that affect the rate of stream erosion.

Figure 1 *The Grand Canyon is located in northwestern Arizona. It formed over millions of years as running water eroded rock and soil. In some places the canyon is 29 km wide.*

Water, Water Everywhere

Have you ever wondered how rivers keep flowing and where rivers get their water? The water cycle answers these and other questions. The **water cycle,** shown on the next page, is the continuous movement of water from water sources, such as lakes or oceans, into the air, onto land, into the ground, and back to the water sources.

The Water Cycle

Condensation occurs when water vapor cools and changes into liquid water droplets that form clouds in the atmosphere.

Precipitation is rain, snow, sleet, or hail that falls from clouds onto the Earth's surface.

Runoff is water that flows across land and collects in rivers, streams, and eventually the ocean.

Evaporation occurs when liquid water from the Earth's surface and from living organisms changes into water vapor.

Infiltration is the movement of water into the ground due to the pull of gravity.

Percolation is the downward movement of water through pores and other spaces in soil due to gravity.

Activity

Imagine that you are planning a rafting trip down the Missouri River to the Mississippi River. On a map of the United States, trace the route of your trip from the Rocky Mountains in Montana to the mouth of the Mississippi River, in Louisiana. What major tributaries would you travel past? What cities would you pass through? Mark them on the map. How many kilometers would you travel on this trip?

TRY at HOME

River Systems

Look at the pattern of lines on the palm of your hand. Notice how some of the smaller lines join together to form larger lines. Now imagine those lines are rivers and streams. The smaller lines would be the streams and tributaries and the larger lines would be rivers. **Tributaries** are smaller streams or rivers that flow into larger ones. Like the network of lines on the palm of your hand, streams and rivers make up a network on land. This network of streams and rivers is called a river system and it drains an area of its runoff.

Drainage Basins River systems are divided into regions known as drainage basins. A **drainage basin,** or *watershed,* is the land drained by a river system, which includes the main river and all of its tributaries. The largest drainage basin in the United States is the Mississippi River basin. It has hundreds of tributaries that extend from the Rocky Mountains, in the West, to the Appalachian Mountains, in the East.

The map in **Figure 2** shows that the Mississippi River drainage basin covers more than one-third of the United States. Other major drainage basins in the United States are the Columbia, Rio Grande, and Colorado River basins.

Divides Drainage basins are separated from each other by an area called a **divide.** A divide is generally an area of higher ground than the basins it separates. On the map below, you can see that the Continental Divide is a major divide in the United States. On which side do you live?

Continental Divide

Figure 2 *The Continental Divide runs through the Rocky Mountains. It separates the drainage basins that flow into the Atlantic Ocean and the Gulf of Mexico from those that flow into the Pacific Ocean.*

Stream Erosion

As a stream forms, it erodes soil and rock to create a channel. A **channel** is the path that a stream follows. At first, stream channels are small and steep. As more rock and soil are transported downstream, the channels become wider and deeper. When streams become longer, they are referred to as rivers. Have you ever wondered why some streams flow faster than others?

Gradient The stream shown in **Figure 3** is flowing down a steep mountain side. This stream has a high gradient. *Gradient* is the measure of the change in elevation over a certain distance. A high gradient gives a stream or river more energy to erode rock and soil. A river or stream with a low gradient, such as the one in **Figure 4,** has less energy for erosion.

Discharge The amount of water a stream or river carries in a given amount of time is called *discharge*. The discharge of a stream increases when a major storm occurs or when warm weather rapidly melts snow. As the stream's discharge increases, its erosive energy, speed, and load increase.

MATH BREAK

Calculating a Stream's Gradient

If a river starts at an elevation of 4,900 m and travels 450 km downstream to a lake that is at an elevation of 400 m, what is the stream's gradient?

Figure 3 *A mountain stream flows rapidly and has more erosive energy.*

Figure 4 *A river on a flat plain flows slowly and has less erosive energy.*

Load The materials carried in a stream's water are collectively called the stream's **load.** The size of the particles in the stream's load is affected by the stream's speed. Fast-moving streams can carry large particles. The load also affects the stream's rate of erosion. Rocks and pebbles bounce and scrape along the bottom and sides of the stream bed. The illustration below shows the three ways a stream can carry its load.

1 A stream can bounce large materials, such as pebbles and boulders, along the stream bed. These rocks are called the **bed load.**

2 A stream can carry small rocks and soil in suspension. These materials, called the **suspended load,** make the river look muddy.

3 Some material is carried in solution, meaning that the material is dissolved in the water. The **dissolved load** consists of dissolved materials, such as sodium and calcium.

✓ Self-Check

What would happen to a suspended load if the river slowed down? *(See page 136 to check your answer.)*

The Stages of a River

In the early 1900s, William Morris Davis developed a model that identified the stages of river development. According to this model, rivers evolve from a youthful stage to an old-age stage. Davis believed that all rivers erode in the same way and at the same rate. Today, however, scientists support a different model that considers the effects of a river's environment on stream development. For example, because different material erodes at different rates, one river may develop more quickly than another river. Many factors, including climate, gradient, and load, influence the development of a river. Although scientists no longer use Davis's model to explain river development, they still use many of his terms to describe a river. Remember, these terms do not tell the actual age of a river. Instead, they are used to describe the general characteristics of the river.

Youthful Rivers A youthful river, like the one shown in **Figure 5,** erodes its channel deeper rather than wider. The river flows quickly because of its steep gradient. Its sides and channel are steep and straight. The river tumbles over rocks in rapids and waterfalls. Youthful rivers have few tributaries.

Mature Rivers A mature river, as shown in **Figure 6,** erodes its channel wider rather than deeper. The gradient of a mature river is not as steep as that of a youthful river, and there are fewer falls and rapids. A mature river is fed by many tributaries, and because of its good drainage, it has more discharge than a younger river.

Figure 5 *This youthful river is located in Yellowstone National Park in Wyoming. The rapids and falls are located where the river flows over hard, resistant rock.*

Figure 6 *A mature river, such as this one in Peru, begins to curve back and forth. The bends in the river's channel are called* meanders.

Figure 7 *This old river is located in New Zealand.*

Old Rivers An old river has a low gradient and extremely low erosive power. Instead of widening and deepening its banks, the river deposits sediment in its channel and along its banks. Old rivers, like the one in **Figure 7,** are characterized by wide, flat *flood plains*, or valleys, and more meanders. Also, an older river has fewer tributaries than a mature river because the smaller tributaries have merged.

Rejuvenated Rivers Rejuvenated rivers occur where the land is raised by the Earth's tectonic forces. When land rises, the river's gradient becomes steeper. The increased gradient of a rejuvenated river allows the river to cut more deeply into the valley floor, as shown in **Figure 8.** Steplike *terraces* often form on both sides of a stream valley as a result of rejuvenation. Terraces are nearly flat portions of the landscape that end at a steep cliff.

Figure 8 *This rejuvenated river is located in Canyonlands National Park, Utah.*

SECTION REVIEW

1. How does the water cycle help to develop river systems?

2. Describe a drainage basin.

3. What are three factors that affect the rate of stream erosion?

4. **Summarizing Data** How do youthful, mature, and old rivers differ?

Terms to Learn

deposition   alluvial fan
alluvium   flood plain
delta

What You'll Do

◆ Describe the different types of stream deposits.
◆ Explain the relationship between rich agricultural regions and river flood plains.

Stream and River Deposits

You have learned that flowing rivers can pick up and move soil and rock. Sooner or later, this material must be deposited somewhere. **Deposition** is the process by which material is dropped, or settles. Imagine a mud puddle after a rainy day. If the water is not disturbed, the soil particles will eventually settle and the muddy water will become clear again. Deposition also forms and renews some of the world's most productive soils. People who live in the lower Mississippi River valley, for example, depend on the river to bring them new, fertile soil.

Deposition in Water

After rivers erode rock and soil, they deposit the rock and soil downstream. Rock and soil deposited by streams is called **alluvium.** Alluvium is dropped at places in a river where the speed of the current decreases. Take a look at **Figure 9** to see how this type of deposition occurs.

Figure 9 *This model illustrates erosion and deposition at a bend, or meander, of a river.*

a Erosion occurs on the outside bank where the water flows faster.

b Deposition occurs along the inside bank where the water flows slower.

Heavy minerals are sometimes deposited at places in a river where the current slows down. This kind of alluvium is called a *placer deposit*. Some placer deposits contain gold, as **Figure 10** shows. During the California gold rush, which began in 1849, many miners panned for gold in the placer deposits of rivers.

Designing a Delta The current also slows when a river empties into a large body of water, such as a lake or an ocean. Much of the river's load may be deposited where the river reaches the large body of water, forming a fan-shaped deposit called a **delta**. In **Figure 11** you can see an astronaut's view of the Nile Delta. A delta usually forms on a flat surface and consists mostly of mud. These mud deposits form new land, causing the coastline to grow.

Figure 10 *Miners rushed to California in the 1850s to find gold. They often found it in the bends of rivers in placer deposits.*

Mediterranean Sea
Nile Delta
Nile River
Egypt

Figure 11 *Alluvium is dropped at the mouth of the Nile River, forming a delta.*

If you look back at the map of the Mississippi River drainage basin in Figure 2, you can see where the Mississippi River flows into the Gulf of Mexico. This is where the Mississippi Delta has formed. Each of the fine mud particles in the delta began its journey far upstream. Parts of Louisiana are made up of particles that were transported from as far away as Montana, Minnesota, Ohio, and Illinois.

Astronomy
CONNECTION

The remains of an ancient riverbed have been discovered on Mars. Satellite images show the deposits of stream channels, which indicate that liquid water once existed on the now dry and frozen planet.

✓ Self-Check

What is one factor that causes the current of a river to slow? *(See page 136 to check your answer.)*

Deposition on Land

When a fast-moving mountain stream flows onto a flat plain, the stream slows down. As the stream slows down, it deposits alluvium where the mountain meets the flat plain, forming an alluvial fan, such as the one shown in **Figure 12.** **Alluvial fans** are fan-shaped deposits that form on dry land.

During periods of high rainfall or rapid snowmelt, a sudden increase in the volume of water flowing into a stream can cause the stream to overflow its banks, flooding the surrounding land. This land is called a **flood plain.** When a stream floods, a layer of alluvium is deposited across the flood plain. Each flood adds another layer of alluvium.

Fatal Flooding Flood plains are very rich farming areas because periodic flooding brings new soil to the land. However, flooding can cause extensive property damage. Much farming activity takes place in the Mississippi River valley, a large flood plain with very rich soil. When the Mississippi River flooded in 1993, however, farms were abandoned and whole towns had to be evacuated. The flood was so huge that it caused damage in nine Midwestern states. **Figure 13** shows an area that was flooded just north of St. Louis, Missouri.

Figure 12 *An alluvial fan, such as this one from the Sierra Nevada, in California, forms when an eroding stream changes rapidly into a depositing stream.*

Figure 13 *The normal flow of the Mississippi River and Missouri River is shown in black. The area that was flooded when both rivers spilled over their banks in 1993 is shaded red.*

SECTION REVIEW

1. What happens to a river's flow that causes alluvium to be deposited?

2. How are alluvial fans and deltas similar? How are they different?

3. Explain why flood plains are good farming areas.

4. **Identifying Relationships** What factors increase the likelihood that alluvium will be deposited?

internet**connect**

SC*i*LINKS
NSTA

TOPIC: Stream Deposits
GO TO: www.scilinks.org
*sci*LINKS NUMBER: HSTE263

Terms to Learn

ground water   permeability
water table   recharge zone
aquifer   artesian spring
porosity

What You'll Do

◆ Identify and describe the location of a water table.
◆ Describe the characteristics of an aquifer.
◆ Explain how caves and sinkholes form as a result of erosion and deposition.

Water Underground

Although we can see surface water in streams and lakes, there is a lot of water flowing underground that we cannot see. The water located within the rocks below the Earth's surface is called **ground water.** Ground water not only is an important resource but also plays an important role in erosion and deposition.

Location of Ground Water

Surface water seeps underground into the soil and rock. Earth scientists divide this underground area into two zones. The upper zone, called the *zone of aeration,* usually is not completely filled with water. The rock and soil that make up this zone are filled with water only immediately after a rain. Farther down, the water accumulates in an area called the *zone of saturation.* Here the spaces between the rock particles are filled with water.

These two zones meet at an underground boundary known as the **water table,** as shown in **Figure 14.** The water table rises during wet seasons and drops during dry seasons. In wet regions the water table can be just beneath the soil's surface or at the surface. But in deserts the water table may be hundreds of meters underground.

Figure 14 *The water table is the upper surface of the zone of saturation.*

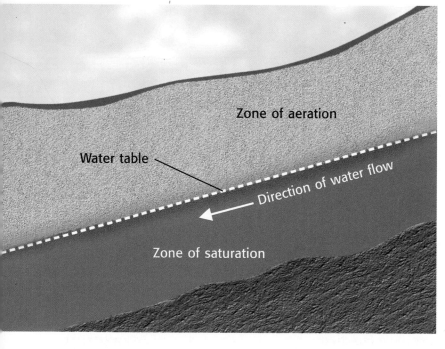

Zone of aeration

Water table

Direction of water flow

Zone of saturation

Aquifers

Some types of rock can hold large quantities of water, while other types can hold little or no water. A rock layer that stores and allows the flow of ground water is called an **aquifer.**

To qualify as an aquifer, a rock layer must be *porous,* or contain open spaces. A rock's **porosity** is the amount of open space between individual rock particles. The rock layer must also allow water to pass freely through it, from one pore to another. If the pores are connected, ground water can flow through the rock layer. A rock's ability to let water pass through it is called **permeability.** A rock that tends to stop the flow of water is impermeable.

Aquifer Geology and Geography The best aquifers are usually formed of sandstone, limestone, or layers of sand and gravel. Some aquifers cover large underground areas and are an important source of water for cities and agriculture. The map in **Figure 15** shows the location of aquifers in the United States.

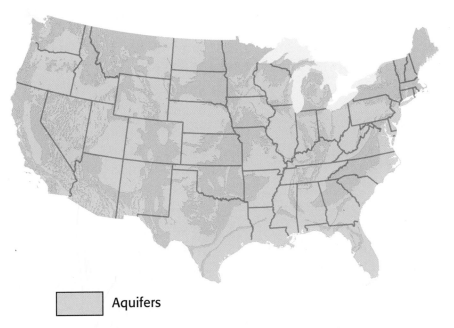

 Aquifers

Figure 15 Aquifers in the Continental United States

Recharge Zones Like rivers, aquifers are dependent on the water cycle to maintain a constant flow of water. The ground surface where water enters an aquifer is called the **recharge zone.** The size of the recharge zone varies depending on how permeable rock is at the surface. In an area that contains a permeable rock layer, the water can seep down into the aquifer. In areas where the aquifer is confined on top by an impermeable rock layer, the recharge zone is restricted to areas where there is a permeable rock layer.

Springs and Wells

Ground-water movement is determined by the slope of the water table. Just like surface water, ground water tends to move downslope, toward lower elevations. If the water table reaches the Earth's surface, water will flow out from the ground, forming a *spring*. Springs are an important source of drinking water. Lakes form in low areas, where the water table is higher than the Earth's surface.

Degree of Permeability

1. Obtain five **plastic-foam cups.**

2. Fill one cup halfway with **soil,** such as garden soil. Pack the soil.

3. Fill a second cup halfway with **sand.** Pack the sand.

4. Poke 5 to 7 holes in the bottom of each cup with a sharpened **pencil.**

5. Fill a third cup with **water.** Hold one of the remaining empty cups under the cup filled with soil. Pour the water into the top cup.

6. Allow the cup to drain for 45 seconds, and then put the cup aside (even if it is still draining). Put the cup filled with water aside.

7. Repeat steps 5 and 6 with the cup of sand. Compare the volumes of the two cups of water. The cup that allowed the most water to pass holds the more permeable sediment.

TRY at HOME

A mud pie the size of a house—where would you see something like that? Turn to page 30 to find out.

Artesian Springs A sloping layer of permeable rock sandwiched between two layers of impermeable rock is called an *artesian formation*. The permeable rock is an aquifer, and the top layer of the impermeable rock is called a *cap rock,* as shown in **Figure 16.** Artesian formations are the source of water for **artesian springs.** Artesian springs are springs that form where cracks occur naturally in the cap rock and the pressurized water in the aquifer flows through the cracks to the surface. Artesian springs are sometimes found in deserts, where they are often the only source of water.

Figure 16 *Artesian springs form when water from an aquifer flows through cracks in the cap rock of an artesian formation.*

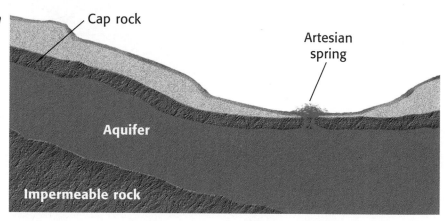

Wells A *well* is a human-made hole that is deeper than the level of the water table; therefore, wells fill with ground water, as shown in **Figure 17.** If a well is not deep enough, it will dry up when the water table falls below the bottom of the well. Also, if too many wells in an area remove ground water too rapidly, the water table will drop and all the wells will run dry.

Figure 17 *A good well is drilled deep enough so that when the water table drops, the well still contains water.*

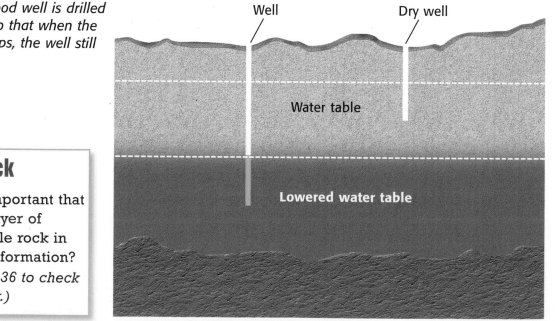

✓ Self-Check

Why is it important that there is a layer of impermeable rock in an artesian formation? *(See page 136 to check your answer.)*

Underground Erosion and Deposition

Unlike a river, which erodes its banks when water moves over rock and soil, ground water erodes certain types of rock by dissolving the rock. Most of the world's caves formed over thousands of years as ground water dissolved limestone. Limestone, which is made of calcium carbonate, dissolves easily in water. As a result, caves form. Some caves reach spectacular proportions, such as the one in **Figure 18.**

Stalactite

Stalagmite

Figure 18 *At Carlsbad Caverns, in New Mexico, underground passages and enormous "rooms" have been eroded below the surface of the Earth.*

Cave Formations While caves are formed by erosion, they also show signs of deposition. Water that drips from a crack in a cave's ceiling leaves behind deposits of calcium carbonate. These deposits of calcium carbonate are a type of limestone called *dripstone*. Water and dissolved limestone can drip downward into sharp, icicle-shaped dripstone features known as a stalactites. At the same time, water drops that fall to the cave's floor add to cone-shaped dripstone features known as stalagmites. If water drips long enough, the stalactites and stalagmites can reach each other and join, forming a dripstone column.

Environment
CONNECTION

Most bat species live in caves. These night-flying mammals navigate by sound and can reach speeds of 95 km/h. Today scientists know that bats play an extremely important role in the environment. Bats are great consumers of insects, and many bat species pollinate plants and distribute seeds.

Sinkholes When the water table is lower than the level of a cave, the cave is no longer supported by the water underneath. The roof of the cave can then collapse, leaving a circular depression called a *sinkhole*. Surface streams can "disappear" into sinkholes and then flow through underground caves. Sinkholes often form lakes in areas where the water table is high. Central Florida is covered with hundreds of round sinkhole lakes. **Figure 19** shows how underground caves can affect a landscape.

Figure 19 *This city block shows the effects of a sinkhole in Winter Park, Florida.*

SECTION REVIEW

1. What is the water table?

2. What is an aquifer?

3. What are some of the features formed by underground erosion and deposition?

4. **Analyzing Relationships** What is the relationship between the zone of aeration, the zone of saturation, and the water table?

Terms to Learn

point-source pollution
nonpoint-source pollution
sewage treatment plant
septic tank

What You'll Do

◆ Describe the stages of treatment for water at a sewage treatment plant.
◆ Compare a septic system with a sewage treatment plant.
◆ Explain how ground water can be both a renewable and a non-renewable resource.

Using Water Wisely

All living things need water to survive. But there is a limited amount of fresh water available on Earth. Only 3 percent of Earth's water is drinkable. And of the 3 percent that is drinkable, 75 percent is frozen in the polar icecaps. That's more than 100 times the volume of water found in the Earth's lakes and streams! This frozen water is not readily available for our use. Therefore, it is important that we use our water resources wisely.

Water Pollution

Surface water, such as rivers and lakes, and ground water are often polluted by waste from cities, factories, and farms. One type of pollution is called **point-source pollution** because it comes from one particular point, such as a sewer pipe or a factory drain. Fortunately, laws prohibit much of this type of pollution.

There is growing concern, however, about another type of pollution, called **nonpoint-source pollution.** This type of pollution, as shown in **Figure 20,** is much more difficult to control because it does not come from a single source. Most nonpoint-source pollution contaminates rivers and lakes by runoff. The main sources of nonpoint-source pollution are street gutters, fertilizers, eroded soils and silt from farming and logging, drainage from mines, and salts from irrigation.

As you know, ground water is an important source of fresh water. In fact, more than half of all household water in the United States comes from ground water. Farms use ground water for irrigation. Because ground water is supplied by water from the Earth's surface, ground water can become contaminated when surface water is polluted. And once polluted, ground water is very difficult to clean up.

Figure 20 *The runoff from this irrigation system could collect pesticides and other pollutants. The result would be nonpoint-source pollution.*

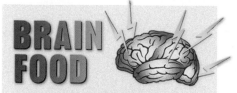
Cleaning Polluted Water

When you flush the toilet or watch water go down the shower drain, do you ever wonder where this water goes? If you live in a city or large town, the water flows through sewer pipes to a sewage treatment plant. **Sewage treatment plants** are factories that clean the waste materials out of water that comes from the sewer or drains. These plants help protect the environment from water pollution. They also protect us from diseases that are easily transmitted through dirty water.

Primary Treatment When water reaches a sewage treatment plant, it is cleaned in two different ways. First it goes through a series of steps known as *primary treatment*. In primary treatment, dirty water is passed through a large screen to catch solid objects, such as paper, rags, and bottle caps. The water is then placed in a large tank, where smaller particles can sink and be filtered out. These particles include things such as food, coffee grounds, and soil. Any floating oils and scum are skimmed off the surface.

Secondary Treatment At this point, the water is ready for *secondary treatment*. In secondary treatment, the water is sent to an aeration tank, where it is mixed with oxygen and bacteria. The bacteria feed on the wastes and use the oxygen. The water is then sent to another settling tank, where chlorine is added to disinfect the water. The water is finally released into a water source—a stream, a lake, or the ocean. **Figure 21** shows the major components of a sewage treatment plant.

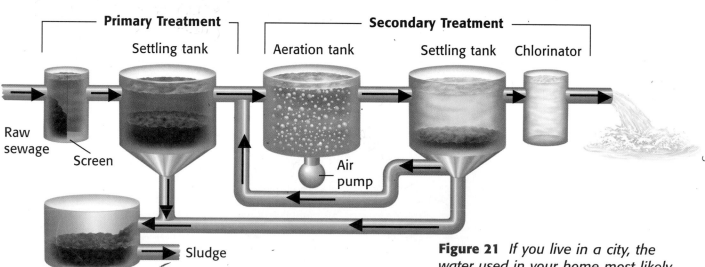

Figure 21 *If you live in a city, the water used in your home most likely ends up at a sewage treatment plant, where it is cleaned by a process that imitates water's natural cleaning cycle.*

Another Way to Clean Waste Water If you live in an area without a sewage treatment plant, your house probably has a septic tank, such as the one shown in **Figure 22.** A **septic tank** is a large underground tank that collects and cleans waste water from a household. Waste water flows from the house into the tank, where the solids sink to the bottom. Bacteria consume these wastes on the bottom of the tank. The water flows from the tank into a group of buried pipes. The buried pipes distribute the water, enabling it to soak into the ground. This group of pipes is called a *drain field*.

Get your hands dirty and learn about some of the methods used to clean up water. Check out page 100 of the LabBook.

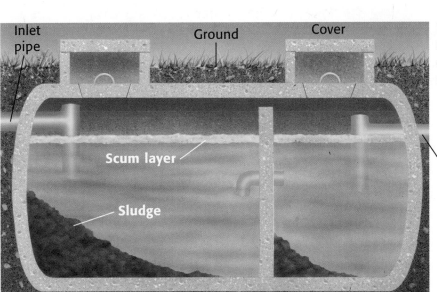

Figure 22 *Most septic tanks must be cleaned out every few years in order to work properly.*

Where the Water Goes

The chart in **Figure 23** shows how an average household in the United States uses water. Notice that less than 8 percent of the water we use in our homes is used for drinking. The rest is used for flushing toilets, doing laundry, bathing, and watering lawns and plants.

Activity

Study the chart at left and determine where the majority of water is used. Think of some ways that you can decrease the amount of water that you use in your home. Share your suggestions with your class.

TRY at HOME

Lawn watering, car washing, and pool maintenance — 32%

Bathing, toilet flushing, and laundry — 60%

Drinking, cooking, washing dishes, running a garbage disposal — 8%

Figure 23 *The average household in the United States uses about 100 gal of water per day. This pie chart shows some common uses of this 100 gal.*

Water in Industry The chart on the previous page shows how fresh water is used in homes. Even more water is required for industry, as shown in **Figure 24.** Water is used to cool power stations, to clean industrial products, to extract minerals, and to create power for factories. Many industries are trying to conserve water by reusing it in their production processes. In the United States, most of the water used in factories is recycled at least once. At least 90 percent of this water can be treated and returned to surface water.

Ground-water supplies also need to be monitored. Although ground water is considered to be a *renewable resource,* a resource that can be replenished, recycling ground water can be a lengthy process. When overused, ground water can sometimes be categorized as a *nonrenewable resource,* a substance that cannot be replaced once it is used. Ground water collects and moves slowly, and water taken from some aquifers might not be replenished for many years.

Figure 24 *The core of a nuclear reactor is cooled by water.*

APPLY

Wasting Water?

How much water do you use when you brush your teeth? Picture yourself at home brushing your teeth. Time how long it takes you to go through the procedure. In your ScienceLog, write down the steps you take, making sure to include how many times you turn on and turn off the faucet. During what percentage of the time spent brushing your teeth is the water running? How do you think you might be wasting water? What are some ways that you could conserve water while brushing your teeth?

Water in Agriculture The Ogallala aquifer is the largest known aquifer in North America. The map in **Figure 25** shows that the Ogallala aquifer runs beneath the ground through eight states, from South Dakota to Texas. For the last 100 years, the aquifer has been used heavily for farming. The Ogallala aquifer provides water for approximately one-fifth of the cropland in the United States. Recently, the water table in the aquifer has dropped so low that some scientists say that it would take at least 1,000 years to replenish the aquifer if it were no longer used.

The Ogallala aquifer can hold enough water to fill Lake Huron. At this time, however, the aquifer is being used 25 times as fast as it is being replenished.

Figure 25 *Because the Ogallala aquifer has been such a good source of ground water, it has become overused. The water table has dropped more than 30 m in some areas.*

Water resources are different from other resources. Because water is necessary for life, there is no alternative resource. Aquifers are often overused and therefore do not have time to replenish themselves. Like surface water, ground water must be conserved.

SECTION REVIEW

1. What is the difference between nonpoint-source and point-source pollution?

2. Summarize the process of water treatment in a sewage treatment plant.

3. What is the difference between a renewable resource and a nonrenewable resource?

4. **Summarizing Data** How does a septic tank work?

internet**connect**

*sci*LINKS.
NSTA

TOPIC: Water Pollution and Conservation
GO TO: www.scilinks.org
*sci*LINKS NUMBER: HSTE270

Making Models Lab

Water Cycle—What Goes Up . . .

Why does a bathroom mirror fog up? Where does water go when it dries up? Where does rain come from, and why don't clouds run out of rain? These questions relate to the major parts of the water cycle—condensation, evaporation, and precipitation. In this activity, you will make a model of the water cycle, and you will watch water as it moves through the model.

MATERIALS

- graduated cylinder
- 50 mL of tap water
- heat-resistant gloves
- beaker
- hot plate
- glass plate or watch glass
- tongs or forceps

Procedure

1 Use the graduated cylinder to pour 50 mL of water into the beaker. Note the water level in the beaker.

2 Put on your safety goggles and gloves. Place the beaker securely on the hot plate. Turn the heat to medium, and bring the water to a boil.

3 While waiting for the water to boil, practice picking up and handling the glass plate or watch glass with the tongs. Hold the glass plate a few centimeters above the beaker, and tilt it so that the lowest edge of the glass is still above the beaker.

4 Observe the glass plate as the water in the beaker boils. In your ScienceLog, write down the changes you see in the beaker, in the air above the beaker, and on the glass plate. Write down any changes you see in the water.

5 Continue until you have observed steam rising off the water, the glass plate becoming foggy, and water dripping from the glass plate.

6 Carefully set the glass plate on a counter or other safe surface as directed by your teacher.

7 Turn off the hot plate, and allow the beaker to cool. If you are directed to do so by your teacher, move the hot beaker with gloves or tongs.

8 In your ScienceLog, copy the illustration shown on the next page. On your sketch, draw and label the water cycle you observed in your model. Include arrows and labels for condensation, evaporation, and precipitation.

Analysis

9 Compare the water level in the beaker now with the water level at the beginning of the experiment. Was there a change? Explain why or why not.

10 If you had used a scale or a balance to measure the mass of the water in the beaker before and after this activity, would the mass have changed? Why or why not?

11 How is your model similar to the Earth's water cycle? On your sketch of the illustration above, label where the processes shown in the model are similar to the Earth's water cycle.

12 When you finished this experiment, the water in the beaker was still hot. What stores much of the energy in the Earth's water cycle?

Going Further

As rainwater runs over the land, the water picks up minerals and salts. Do these minerals and salts evaporate, condense, and precipitate as part of the water cycle? Where do they go?

If the average global temperature on Earth becomes warmer, how would you expect sea levels to change, and why? What if the average global temperature cools?

Chapter Highlights

Vocabulary

erosion *(p. 4)*

water cycle *(p. 4)*

tributary *(p. 6)*

drainage basin *(p. 6)*

divide *(p. 6)*

channel *(p. 7)*

load *(p. 8)*

Section Notes

- Erosion is the removal and transport of soil and rock.

- The water cycle is the continuous movement of water from water sources into the air, onto land, and back into water sources.

- A drainage basin, or watershed, includes a main river and all of its tributaries.

- The rate of stream erosion is affected by many factors, including the stream's gradient, discharge, speed, and load.

- Gradient is the change in elevation over distance.

- Discharge is the volume of water moved by a stream in a given amount of time.

- A stream's load is the material a stream can carry.

- Rivers can be described as youthful, mature, old, or rejuvenated.

Vocabulary

deposition *(p. 11)*

alluvium *(p. 11)*

delta *(p. 12)*

alluvial fan *(p. 13)*

flood plain *(p. 13)*

Section Notes

- Deposition occurs when eroded soil and rock are dropped.

- Alluvium is the material deposited by rivers and streams.

- Deltas are deposits of alluvium at a river's mouth.

- Alluvial fans are deposits of alluvium at the base of a mountain.

- Flood plains are rich farming areas because flooding brings new soils to the area.

☑ Skills Check

Math Concepts

A STREAM'S GRADIENT One factor that can affect the speed of a river is its gradient. The gradient is a measure of the change in elevation over a certain distance. You can use the following equation to calculate a stream's gradient:

$$\text{gradient} = \frac{\text{change in elevation}}{\text{distance}}$$

For example, consider a river that starts at an elevation of 5,500 m and travels 350 km downstream to a lake, which is at an elevation of 2,000 m. By using the formula above, you would find the stream's gradient to be 10 m/km.

$$10 \text{ m/km} = \frac{(5,500 \text{ m} - 2,000 \text{ m})}{350 \text{ km}}$$

Visual Understanding

A STREAM'S LOAD Look back at the diagram on page 8 to review the different types of loads a stream can carry.

A SEWAGE TREATMENT PLANT Study Figure 21 on page 20 to review the two processes used to clean water in a sewage treatment plant.

SECTION 3

Vocabulary

ground water *(p. 14)*

water table *(p. 14)*

aquifer *(p. 14)*

porosity *(p. 14)*

permeability *(p. 14)*

recharge zone *(p. 15)*

artesian spring *(p. 16)*

Section Notes

- Ground water is located below the Earth's surface.

- Ground water can dissolve rock, especially limestone.

- The zone of aeration and the zone of saturation meet at a boundary called the water table.

- An aquifer is a porous and permeable rock layer through which ground water flows.

- A sinkhole forms when the water table is lower than the roof of an underground cave.

SECTION 4

Vocabulary

point-source pollution *(p. 19)*

nonpoint-source pollution *(p. 19)*

sewage treatment plant *(p. 20)*

septic tank *(p. 21)*

Section Notes

- Sewage is treated in sewage treatment plants and in septic tanks.

- In a sewage treatment plant, water is cleaned in two different ways—primary treatment and secondary treatment.

- While water is generally considered to be a renewable resource, when overused it can sometimes be categorized as a nonrenewable resource.

Labs

Clean Up Your Act *(p. 100)*

---

internet**connect**

GO TO: go.hrw.com

Visit the **HRW** Web site for a variety of learning tools related to this chapter. Just type in the keyword:

KEYWORD: HSTDEP

GO TO: www.scilinks.org

Visit the **National Science Teachers Association** on-line Web site for Internet resources related to this chapter. Just type in the *sci*LINKS number for more information about the topic:

TOPIC:	*sci*LINKS NUMBER:
The Grand Canyon	HSTE255
Rivers and Streams	HSTE260
Stream Deposits	HSTE263
Water Underground	HSTE265
Water Pollution and Conservation	HSTE270

Chapter Review

For each set of terms, identify the term that doesn't belong, and explain why.

1. tributary/river/water table

2. load/recharge zone/aquifer

3. delta/alluvial fan/divide

4. porosity/permeability/deposition

5. point-source pollution/nonpoint-source pollution/septic tank

6. primary treatment/secondary treatment/drainage basin

UNDERSTANDING CONCEPTS

Multiple Choice

7. Which of the following processes is not part of the water cycle?
   a. evaporation
   c. condensation
   b. infiltration
   d. deposition

8. Which type of stream load makes a river look muddy?

   a. bed load
   b. dissolved load
   c. suspended load
   d. gravelly load

9. What features are common in youthful river channels?
   a. meanders
   b. flood plains
   c. rapids
   d. sandbars

10. Which depositional feature is found at the coast?
    a. delta
    c. alluvial fan
    b. flood plain
    d. placer deposit

11. Caves are mainly a product of
    a. erosion by rivers.
    b. river deposition.
    c. water pollution.
    d. erosion by ground water.

12. The largest drainage basin in the United States is the

    a. Amazon.
    b. Columbia.
    c. Colorado.
    d. Mississippi.

13. An aquifer must be
    a. nonporous and nonpermeable.
    b. nonporous and permeable.
    c. porous and nonpermeable.
    d. porous and permeable.

14. Which of the following is a point source of water pollution?
    a. fertilizer from a farming area
    b. runoff from city streets
    c. a wastewater pipe
    d. leaking septic tanks

15. During primary treatment at a sewage treatment plant,
    a. water is sent to an aeration tank.
    b. water is mixed with bacteria and oxygen.
    c. dirty water is passed through a large screen.
    d. water is sent to a settling tank where chlorine is added.

Short Answer

16. What is the relationship between tributaries and rivers?

17. How are aquifers replenished?

18. Why are caves usually found in limestone-rich regions?

Concept Mapping

19. Use the following terms to create a concept map: zone of aeration, zone of saturation, water table, gravity, porosity, permeability.

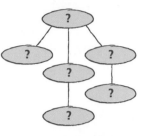

CRITICAL THINKING AND PROBLEM SOLVING

Write one or two sentences to answer the following questions:

20. What role does water play in erosion and deposition?

21. What are the features of a river channel that has a steep gradient?

22. Why is ground water hard to clean up?

23. Imagine you are hiking beside a mature stream. What would the stream be like?

24. How can water be considered both a renewable and a nonrenewable resource? Give an example of each case.

MATH IN SCIENCE

25. A sinkhole has formed in a town with a population of 5,000. The town is declared a disaster area, and $2 million is given to the town by the federal government. The local government uses 60 percent of the money for repairs to city property, and the rest is given to the townspeople.
    a. How much would each person receive?
    b. If there are 2,000 families in the town, how much would each family receive?
    c. Would each family receive enough money to help them rebuild a home? If not, how could the money be distributed more fairly?

INTERPRETING GRAPHICS

The hydrograph below illustrates river flow over a period of 1 year. The discharge readings are from the Yakima River, in Washington. The Yakima River flows eastward from the Cascade Mountains to the Columbia River.

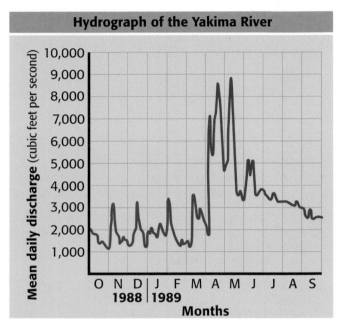

Hydrograph of the Yakima River

26. In which months is there the highest river discharge?

27. Why is there such a high river discharge during these months?

28. What might cause the peaks in river discharge between November and March?

Reading Check-up

Take a minute to review your answers to the Pre-Reading Questions found at the bottom of page 2. Have your answers changed? If necessary, revise your answers based on what you have learned since you began this chapter.

BUBBLE, BOIL, & SQUIRT

In parts of Yellowstone National Park boiling water blasts into the sky, lakes of strange-colored mud boil and gurgle, and hot gases hiss from the ground. What are these strange geologic features? What causes them? The story begins deep in the Earth.

Old Geysers

One of Yellowstone's main tourist attractions is a *geyser* called Old Faithful. Erupting every 60 to 70 minutes, Old Faithful sends a plume of steam and scalding-hot water as high as 60 m into the air. A geyser is formed when a narrow vent connects one or more underground chambers to Earth's surface. These underground chambers are heated by nearly molten rock. As underground water flows into the vent and chambers, it is heated above 100°C. The superheated water quickly turns to steam and explodes first toward the surface and then into the air. And Old Faithful erupts right on schedule!

Nature's Hot Tub

A *hot spring* is a geyser without pressure. Its vents are wider than a geyser's, and they let the underground water cool a little and flow to the surface rather than erupt in a big fountain. To be called a hot spring, the water must be at least as warm as human body temperature (37°C). Some underground springs are several hundred degrees Celsius.

Flying Mud Pies

Mud pots form when steam or hot underground water trickles to the surface and chemically weathers and dissolves surface features, such as rocks. The mixture of dissolved rock and water creates a boiling,

bubbling pool of sticky liquid clay. But don't get too close! Occasionally, the steam will rise quickly and forcefully enough to make the mud pot behave like a volcano. When it does, a mud pot can toss car-sized gobs of mud high into the air!

Some mud pots become *paint pots* when microorganisms or brightly colored minerals are mixed in. For instance, if there is a lot of iron in the mud, the paint pot will turn reddish brown or yellowish brown. Other minerals and bacteria can make the mud white or bluish in color. Some paint pots may even gurgle up blobs in several different colors.

▲ *Mud Pot in Yellowstone National Park*

What Do You Think?

▶ Some people believe that tapping geothermal energy sources such as geysers could harm the delicate ecology of those sources. Find out about the benefits and the risks of using geothermal energy. What is your opinion?

EYE ON THE ENVIRONMENT

Disaster Along the Delta

As the sun rises over the delta wetlands of the Mississippi River, fishermen test their skills. Long-legged birds step lightly through the marsh, hunting fish or frogs for breakfast. And hundreds of species of plants and animals start another day in this fragile ecosystem. But the delta ecosystem is in danger of being destroyed.

The threat comes from efforts to make the Mississippi more useful. Large portions of the river bottom were dredged to make the river deeper for ship traffic. Underwater channels were built to control flooding. What no one realized was that sediments that were once deposited to form new land now pass through the deep channels and flow out into the ocean.

Those river sediments replaced the land that was lost every year to erosion. Without the sediments, the river can't replace the land lost to erosion. And so the Mississippi River delta is disappearing. By 1995, more than half the wetlands were already gone, swept out to sea by waves along the Louisiana coast.

▲ *The Mississippi River flows from Minnesota through the Midwest to the Gulf of Mexico in the southern United States.*

Sedimental Journey

The Mississippi River journeys 3,766 km to empty 232 million metric tons of sediment into the Gulf of Mexico each year. The end of the Mississippi River delta forms the largest area of wetlands in North America. A *delta* forms when sediments settle at the mouth of a river. At the Mississippi River delta, the sediments build up and form new land along the Louisiana coastline. The area around the delta is called *wetlands.* It has fertile soil, which produces many crops, and a variety of habitats—marsh, freshwater, and saltwater—that support many species of plants and animals.

Taking Action to Preserve the Delta

Since the mid-1980s, local, state, and federal governments, along with Louisiana citizens and businesses, have been working together to monitor and restore the Mississippi River delta. Some projects to protect the delta include filling in canals that divert the sediments and even using old Christmas trees as fences to trap the sediments! With the continued efforts of scientists, government leaders, and concerned citizens, the Mississippi River delta stands a good chance of recovering.

Explore the Delta

▶ Find out more about the industries and organisms that depend on the Mississippi River delta for survival. What will happen to them if we don't take care of the ecosystem?

Exploring the Oceans

Pre-Reading Questions

1. How have Earth's oceans changed over time?

2. Name two ways to study the ocean without going under water.

3. Name two valuable resources that are taken from the ocean.

EXIT ONLY?

To study what life under water would be like, scientists sometimes live in underwater laboratories. How do these scientists enter and leave these labs? Believe it or not, the simplest way is through a hole in the lab's floor. You might think water would come in through the hole, but it doesn't. People inside the lab can breathe freely and can come and go through the hole at any time. How is this possible? Do the following activity to find out.

Procedure

1. Fill a **large bowl** about two-thirds full of **water.**

2. Turn a **clear plastic cup** upside down.

3. Slowly guide the cup straight down into the water. Be careful not to tip the cup.

4. Record your observations in your ScienceLog.

Analysis

5. How does the air inside the cup affect the water below the cup?

6. How do your findings relate to the hole in the bottom of the underwater research lab?

A New World Under Water

Seventy-one percent of the Earth's surface is covered by ocean water. However, large portions of the oceans, especially the deepest parts and the parts nearest the poles, remain completely unexplored. In the past several decades, new technologies have made underwater exploration possible, allowing scientists to gather important information about the Earth's greatest resource. In this chapter, you'll learn about the fascinating world under the water and the important part the oceans play in making our planet livable.

Terms to Learn

salinity
thermocline
water cycle

What You'll Do

◆ Name the major divisions of the global ocean.
◆ Describe the history of Earth's oceans.
◆ Summarize the properties and other aspects of ocean water.
◆ Summarize the interaction between the ocean and the atmosphere.

Earth's Oceans

Earth stands out from the other planets in our solar system primarily for one reason—71 percent of the Earth's surface is covered with water. Most of Earth's water is found in the global ocean, which is divided by the continents into four main oceans. This is shown in the figure below. The ocean is a unique body of water that plays many roles in regulating Earth's environment. Read on to learn more about one of our most important resources—the ocean.

Divisions of the Global Ocean

Arctic Ocean The Arctic Ocean is the smallest ocean. This ocean is unique because much of it is covered by ice. Scientists are just beginning to successfully explore the frozen world of the Arctic Ocean.

Indian Ocean The Indian Ocean is the third largest ocean. Part of the longest mountain range in the world, the mid-ocean ridge, runs along the floor of the Indian Ocean.

Atlantic Ocean The volume of the Atlantic Ocean is about half that of the Pacific.

Pacific Ocean The largest ocean is the Pacific Ocean. It is a vast body of water that has enough water to fill 1,200,000,000,000,000,000 bathtubs!

How Did the Oceans Form?

About four and a half billion years ago, the Earth was a very different place. There were no oceans. Volcanoes spewed lava, ash, and gases all over the planet, which was much hotter than it is today. The volcanic gases, including water vapor, began to form Earth's atmosphere. While the atmosphere developed, the Earth was cooling. Sometime before 4 billion years ago, the Earth cooled enough for water vapor to condense and fall as rain. The rain began filling the lower levels of Earth's surface, and the first oceans began to form.

Earth's oceans have changed a lot throughout history. Scientists who study oceans have learned much about the oceans' history, as shown in the diagram below.

✓ Self-Check

Examine the diagram below. If North America and South America continue to drift westward and Asia continues to drift eastward, what will eventually happen? *(See page 136 to check your answer.)*

The Recent History of Earth's Oceans

About 245 million years ago, the continents were one giant landmass called *Pangaea* and the oceans were one giant water body called *Panthalassa.*

About 180 million years ago, the North Atlantic Ocean and the Indian Ocean began to form.

About 65 million years ago, the South Atlantic Ocean was much smaller than it is today.

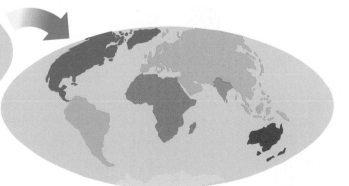

Today the continents continue to move at a rate of 1–10 cm per year. While the Pacific Ocean is getting smaller, the other oceans are expanding.

Characteristics of Ocean Water

You know that ocean water is different from the water that flows from the faucet of your kitchen sink. For one thing, ocean water is not safe to drink. But there are other characteristics that make ocean water special.

Ocean Water Is Salty Have you ever swallowed a mouthful of water while swimming in the ocean? It sure had a nasty taste, didn't it? Most of the salt in the ocean is the same kind of salt that we sprinkle on our food. Scientists call this salt *sodium chloride*.

The ocean is so salty because salt has been added to it for billions of years. As rivers and streams flow toward the oceans, they dissolve various minerals on land. The running water carries these dissolved minerals to the ocean. At the same time, water is *evaporating* from the ocean, leaving the dissolved solids behind. The most abundant dissolved solid in the ocean is sodium chloride, a compound of the elements sodium (Na) and chlorine (Cl), as shown in **Figure 1.**

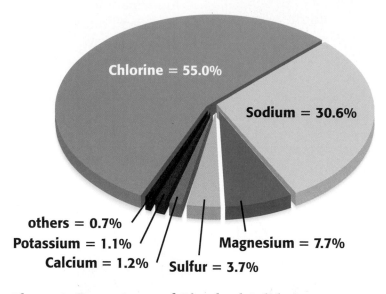

Figure 1 Percentages of Dissolved Solids in Ocean Water *This pie chart shows the relative amounts of the dissolved solids in ocean water.*

Chlorine = 55.0%
Sodium = 30.6%
others = 0.7%
Potassium = 1.1%
Calcium = 1.2%
Sulfur = 3.7%
Magnesium = 7.7%

Chock-full of Solids If more water evaporates than enters the ocean, the ocean's salinity increases. **Salinity** is a measure of the amount of dissolved salts and other solids in a given amount of liquid. Salinity is usually measured as grams of dissolved solids per kilogram of water. Think of it this way: 1 kg (1,000 g) of ocean water contains 35 g of dissolved solids on average. Therefore, if you evaporated 1 kg of ocean water, about 35 g of solids would remain.

Factors That Affect Salinity Some areas of the ocean are saltier than others. Coastal water in areas with hotter, drier climates typically have a higher salinity than coastal water in cooler, more humid areas. This is because less fresh water runs into the ocean in drier areas and because heat increases the evaporation rate. Evaporation removes water but leaves salts and other dissolved solids behind. Also, coastal areas where major rivers run into the ocean have a relatively low salinity. In these areas, the rivers add to the ocean large volumes of fresh water, which contains fewer dissolved solids than sea water.

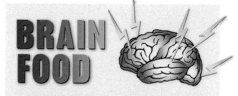

Did you know that there are about 9 million tons of gold dissolved in the ocean? Too bad the gold's concentration is only 0.000004 mg per kilogram of sea water. Mining the gold from the water would be difficult, and the cost of removing it would be greater than the gold's value.

Another factor that affects ocean salinity is water movement. Surface water in some areas of the ocean, such as bays, gulfs, and seas, circulates less than surface water in other parts. Areas in the open ocean that have no currents running through them can also be slow moving. **Figure 2** shows how salinity variations relate to many factors.

Temperature Zones The temperature of ocean water decreases as the depth of the water increases. However, this does not occur gradually from the ocean's surface to its bottom. Water in the ocean can be divided into three layers according to temperature. As you can see in the graph below, the water at the top is much warmer than the average temperature of the ocean.

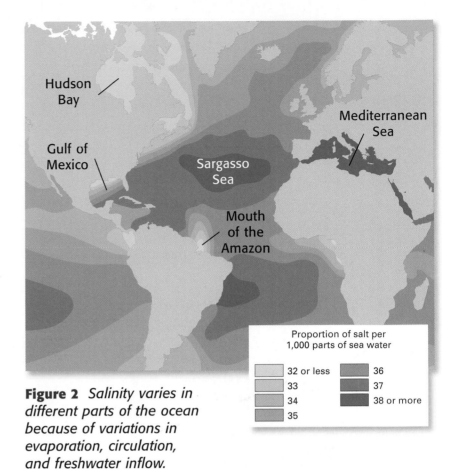

Figure 2 *Salinity varies in different parts of the ocean because of variations in evaporation, circulation, and freshwater inflow.*

Proportion of salt per 1,000 parts of sea water

32 or less		36	
33		37	
34		38 or more	
35			

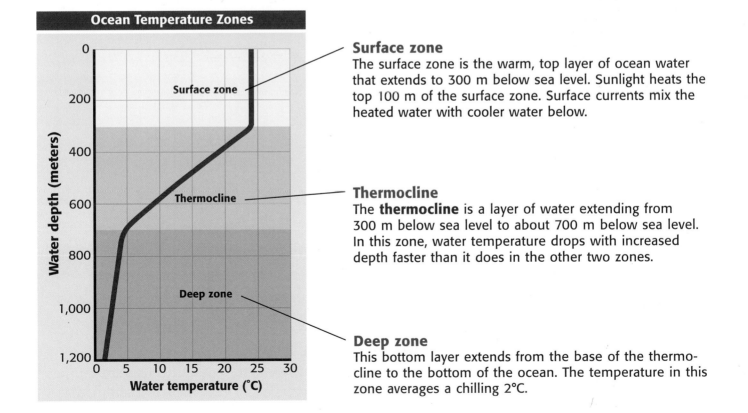

Surface zone
The surface zone is the warm, top layer of ocean water that extends to 300 m below sea level. Sunlight heats the top 100 m of the surface zone. Surface currents mix the heated water with cooler water below.

Thermocline
The **thermocline** is a layer of water extending from 300 m below sea level to about 700 m below sea level. In this zone, water temperature drops with increased depth faster than it does in the other two zones.

Deep zone
This bottom layer extends from the base of the thermocline to the bottom of the ocean. The temperature in this zone averages a chilling 2°C.

Surface Temperature Changes Temperatures in the surface zone vary with latitude and the time of year. Surface temperatures range from 1°C near the poles to about 24°C near the equator. Areas of the ocean along the equator are warmer because they receive more sunlight per year than areas closer to the poles. However, the sun's rays in the Northern Hemisphere are more direct during the summer than during the winter. Therefore, the surface zone absorbs more thermal energy during the summer.

If you live near the coast, you may know firsthand how different a dip in the ocean feels in December than it feels in July. **Figure 3** shows how surface-zone temperatures vary depending on the time of year.

Figure 3 *These satellite images show that the surface temperatures in the northern Pacific Ocean change with the seasons.*

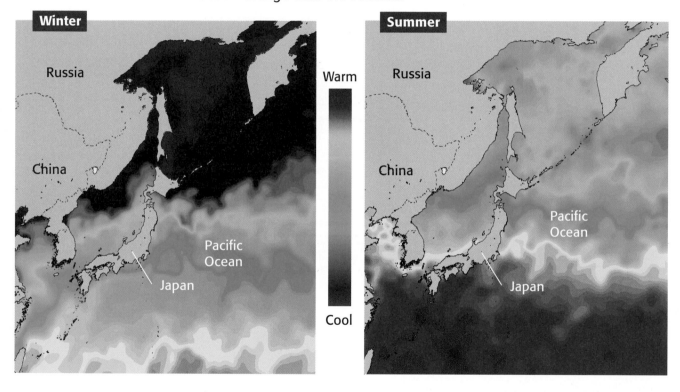

internet connect

SC*i*LINKS.
NSTA

TOPIC: Exploring Earth's Oceans
GO TO: www.scilinks.org
*sci*LINKS NUMBER: HSTE305

SECTION REVIEW

1. Name the major divisions of the global ocean.

2. Explain how Earth's first oceans formed.

3. **Summarizing Data** List three factors that affect salinity in the ocean and three factors that affect ocean temperatures. Explain how each factor affects salinity or temperature.

The Ocean and the Water Cycle

If you could sit on the moon and look down at Earth, what would you see? You would notice that Earth's surface is made up of three basic components—water, land, and air. All three are involved in an ongoing process called the water cycle, as shown below. The **water cycle** is a cycle that links all of Earth's solid, liquid, and gaseous water together. The ocean is an important part of the water cycle because nearly all of Earth's water is found in the ocean.

Condensation As water vapor rises into the atmosphere, it cools and mixes with dust particles. Eventually, the water vapor turns to liquid water on the dust particles. This change from a gas to a liquid is called **condensation.**

Precipitation As droplets of water move inside clouds, the droplets collide and stick together, forming larger, heavier droplets. These droplets then fall back to Earth's surface in the form of precipitation. **Precipitation** is solid or liquid water that falls to Earth. Most precipitation falls directly back into the ocean because the ocean covers most of Earth's surface.

Evaporation The sun heats liquid water, causing it to rise into the atmosphere as water vapor. This physical change from a liquid to a gas is called **evaporation.** Water evaporates directly from oceans, lakes, rivers, falling rain, and other sources.

A Global Thermostat

The ocean plays a vital role in maintaining conditions favorable for life on Earth. Perhaps the most important function of the ocean is to absorb and hold energy from sunlight. This function regulates temperatures in the atmosphere.

A Hot Exchange The ocean absorbs and releases thermal energy much more slowly than dry land does. If it were not for this function of the ocean, the average air temperature on Earth would vary from above 100°C during the day to below –100°C at night. This rapid exchange of energy between the atmosphere and the Earth's surface would cause violent weather patterns. Life as we know it could not exist with these unstable conditions.

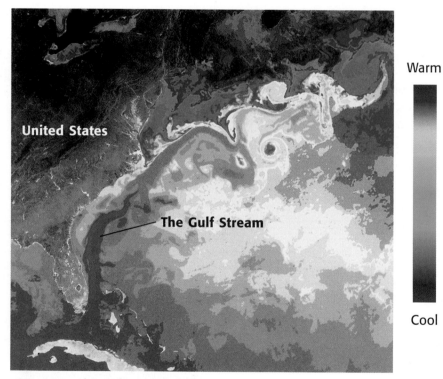

United States

The Gulf Stream

Warm

Cool

Figure 4 *This infrared satellite image shows the Gulf Stream moving warm water from lower latitudes to higher latitudes.*

Have Heat, Will Travel The ocean also regulates temperatures on a more local scale. At the equator, the sun's rays are more direct, which causes equatorial waters to be warmer than waters at higher latitudes. But currents in the oceans circulate water, as well as the energy it contains, as shown in **Figure 4.** This circulation of warm water causes some coastal lands to have warmer climates than they would have without the currents. The British Isles, for example, have a warmer climate than most regions at the same latitude because of the warm water of the Gulf Stream.

SECTION REVIEW

1. Why is the ocean an important part of the water cycle?

2. Between which two steps of the water cycle does the ocean fit?

3. **Making Inferences** Explain why St. Louis, Missouri, has colder winters and warmer summers than San Francisco, California, even though the two cities are at about the same latitude.

Terms to Learn

continental shelf	mid-ocean ridge
continental slope	rift valley
continental rise	seamount
abyssal plain	ocean trench

What You'll Do

◆ Identify the two major regions of the ocean floor.

◆ Classify subdivisions and features of the two major regions of the ocean floor.

◆ Describe technologies for studying the ocean floor.

Science

CONNECTION

Turn to page 66 to meet the most famous underwater explorer who ever lived.

The Ocean Floor

What lies at the bottom of the ocean? How deep is the ocean? These are questions that were once unanswerable. But humans have learned a lot about the ocean floor, especially in the last few decades. Using state-of-the-art technology, scientists have discovered a wide variety of landforms on the ocean floor. Scientists have also determined accurate depths for almost the entire ocean floor.

Exploring the Ocean Floor

Some parts of the ocean are so deep that humans must use special underwater vessels to travel there. Perhaps the most familiar underwater vessel used by scientists to study the ocean floor is the minisub called *Alvin*. Scientists have used *Alvin* for many underwater missions, including searches for sunken ships, the recovery of a lost hydrogen bomb, and explorations of landforms on the sea floor.

Although the use of *Alvin* has enabled scientists to make some amazing discoveries, scientists are developing new vessels for ocean exploration, such as an underwater airplane called *Deep Flight*. This vessel, shown in **Figure 5,** moves through the water much like an airplane moves through the air. Future models of *Deep Flight* will be designed to transport pilots to the deepest part of the ocean.

Figure 5 *Like the Wright brothers' first successful airplane,* Deep Flight *sets the stage for a bright future— this time in underwater "flight."*

Revealing the Ocean Floor

What if you were an explorer assigned to map uncharted areas on the planet? You might think there were not many uncharted areas left because most of the land had already been explored. But what about the bottom of the ocean? If you could travel to the bottom of the ocean in *Deep Flight,* you would see the world's largest mountain chain and canyons deeper than the Grand Canyon. And because it is under water, much of this area is unexplored.

As you began your descent into the underwater realm, you would notice two major regions—the *continental margin,* which is made of continental crust, and the *deep-ocean basin,* which is made of oceanic crust. It may help to imagine the ocean as a giant swimming pool; the continental margin is the shallow end and slope of the pool, and the deep-ocean basin is the deep end of the pool. **Figure 6** shows how these two regions are subdivided.

Figure 6 *The continental margin is subdivided into three depth zones, and the deep-ocean basin consists of one depth zone with several features.*

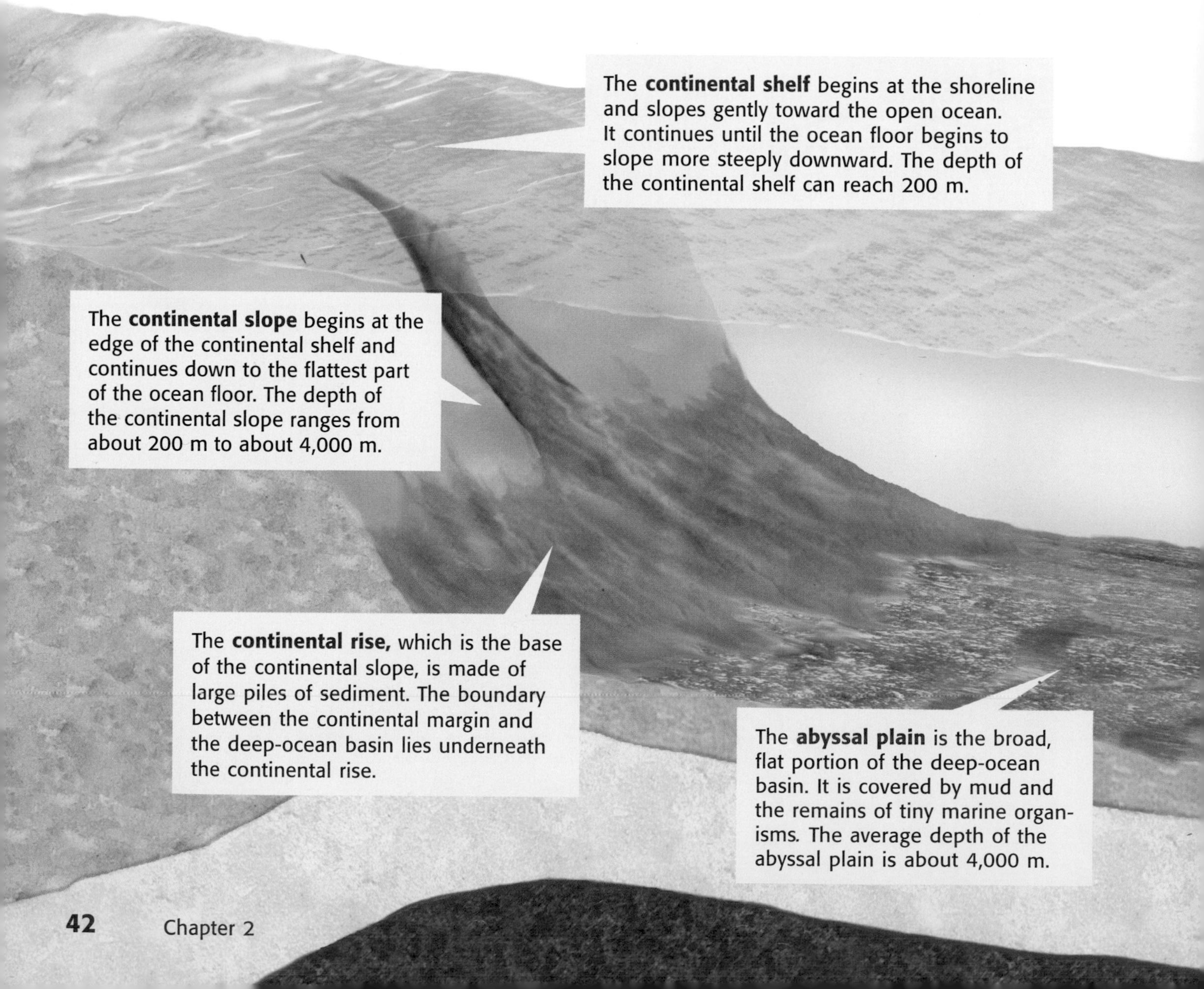

The **continental shelf** begins at the shoreline and slopes gently toward the open ocean. It continues until the ocean floor begins to slope more steeply downward. The depth of the continental shelf can reach 200 m.

The **continental slope** begins at the edge of the continental shelf and continues down to the flattest part of the ocean floor. The depth of the continental slope ranges from about 200 m to about 4,000 m.

The **continental rise,** which is the base of the continental slope, is made of large piles of sediment. The boundary between the continental margin and the deep-ocean basin lies underneath the continental rise.

The **abyssal plain** is the broad, flat portion of the deep-ocean basin. It is covered by mud and the remains of tiny marine organisms. The average depth of the abyssal plain is about 4,000 m.

Underwater Real Estate As you can see, the continental margin is subdivided into the continental shelf, the continental slope, and the continental rise based on depth and changes in slope. The deep-ocean basin consists of the abyssal plain, with features such as mid-ocean ridges, rift valleys, and ocean trenches that form near the boundaries of Earth's *tectonic plates*. On parts of the abyssal plain that are not near plate boundaries, thousands of seamounts are found on the ocean floor.

> ## ✔ Self-Check
>
> How do the locations of rift valleys and ocean trenches differ? *(See page 136 to check your answer.)*

(See page 136 to check your answer.)

Activity

To get an idea of how deep parts of the ocean are, use an encyclopedia to find out how deep the Grand Canyon is. Compare this depth with that of the Mariana Trench, which is more than 11,000 m deep! Make a model of this difference using clay, or draw a graph of this difference to scale.

TRY at HOME

---

internetconnect

SCiLINKS
NSTA

TOPIC: The Ocean Floor
GO TO: www.scilinks.com
sciLINKS NUMBER: HSTE310

Mid-ocean ridges are mountain chains formed where *tectonic plates* pull apart. This pulling motion creates cracks in the ocean floor called *rift zones.* As plates pull apart, magma rises to fill in the spaces. Heat from the magma causes the crust on either side of the rifts to expand, forming the ridges.

Seamounts are individual mountains of volcanic material. They form where magma pushes its way through or between tectonic plates. If a seamount builds up above sea level, it becomes a volcanic island.

As mountains build up, a **rift valley** forms between them in the rift zone.

Ocean trenches are seemingly bottomless cracks in the deep-ocean basin. Ocean trenches form where one oceanic plate is forced underneath a continental plate or another oceanic plate.

MATH BREAK

Depths of the Deep

The depths in a bathymetric profile are calculated using the following simple formula:

$$D = \frac{1}{2}t \times v$$

D is the depth of the ocean floor, t is the time it takes for the sound to reach the bottom and return to the surface, and v equals the speed of sound in water (1,500 m/s). Calculate D for the following three parts of the ocean floor:

1. a mid-ocean ridge ($t = 2$ s)
2. an ocean trench ($t = 14$ s)
3. an abyssal plain ($t = 5.3$ s)

Viewing the Ocean Floor from Above

In spite of the great success of underwater exploration, sending scientists into deep water is still risky. Fortunately, there are ways to survey the underwater realm from the surface and from high above in space. Read on to learn about two technologies—sonar and satellites—that enable scientists to study the ocean floor without going below the surface.

Seeing by Sonar   *Sonar*, which stands for "sound navigation and ranging," is a technology based on the echo-ranging behavior of bats. Scientists use sonar to determine the ocean's depth by sending high-frequency sound pulses from a ship down into the ocean. The sound travels through the water, bounces off the ocean floor, and returns to the ship. The deeper the water is, the longer the round trip takes. Scientists then calculate the depth by multiplying half the travel time by the speed of sound in water (about 1,500 m/s). This process is shown in the illustration below.

1 To map a section of the ocean floor, scientists travel by ship across the ocean's surface, repeatedly sending sonar signals to the ocean floor.

2 The longer it takes for the sound to bounce off the ocean floor and return to the ship, the deeper the floor is in that spot.

3 Scientists plot sonar signals to make a *bathymetric profile,* which is basically a map of the ocean floor showing its depth variations.

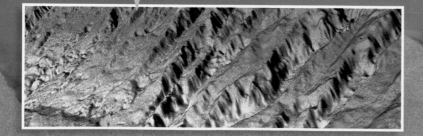

Oceanography via Satellite In the 1970s, scientists began studying Earth from satellites in orbit around the Earth. In 1978, scientists launched the satellite *Seasat.* This satellite focused on the ocean, sending images back to Earth that allowed scientists to measure the direction and speed of ocean currents.

Geosat, once a top-secret military satellite, has been used to measure slight changes in the height of the ocean's surface. Different underwater features, such as mountains and trenches, affect the height of the water above them, thus reflecting the underwater topography of the ocean floor. Scientists measure the different heights of the ocean surface and use the measurements to make highly detailed maps of the ocean floor. As illustrated in **Figure 7,** oceanographers can make maps that cover a lot more territory by using satellites than by using ship-based sonar readings.

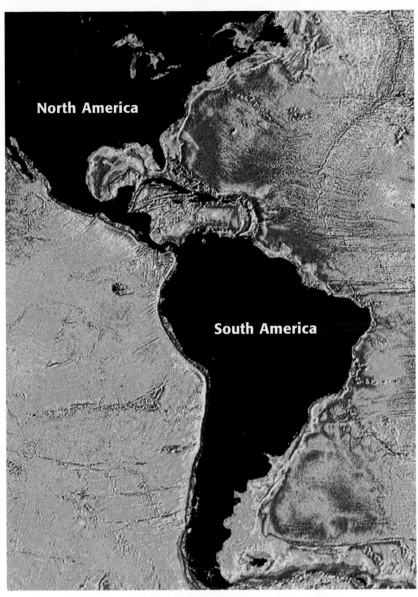

Figure 7 *The map above was generated by satellite measurements of different heights of the ocean surface.*

SECTION REVIEW

1. Name the two major regions of the ocean floor.

2. List the subdivisions of the continental margin.

3. List three technologies for studying the ocean floor, and explain how they are used.

4. **Interpreting Graphics** What part of the ocean floor would the bathymetric profile at right represent?

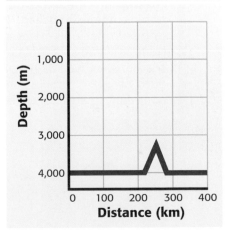

Terms to Learn

plankton   benthic environment
nekton   pelagic environment
benthos

What You'll Do

◆ Identify and describe the three groups of marine organisms.
◆ Identify and describe the benthic and pelagic environments.
◆ Classify the zones of the benthic and pelagic environments.

Life in the Ocean

The ocean contains a wide variety of life-forms, many of which we know little about. Trying to study them can be quite a challenge for scientists. To make things easier, scientists classify marine organisms into three main groups. Scientists also divide the ocean into two main environments based on the types of organisms that live in them. These two main environments are further subdivided into ecological zones based on locations of different organisms.

The Three Groups of Marine Life

The three main groups of marine life are plankton, nekton, and benthos. Marine organisms are placed into one of these three groups according to where they live and how they move. Carefully examine the figure below to understand the differences between these groups.

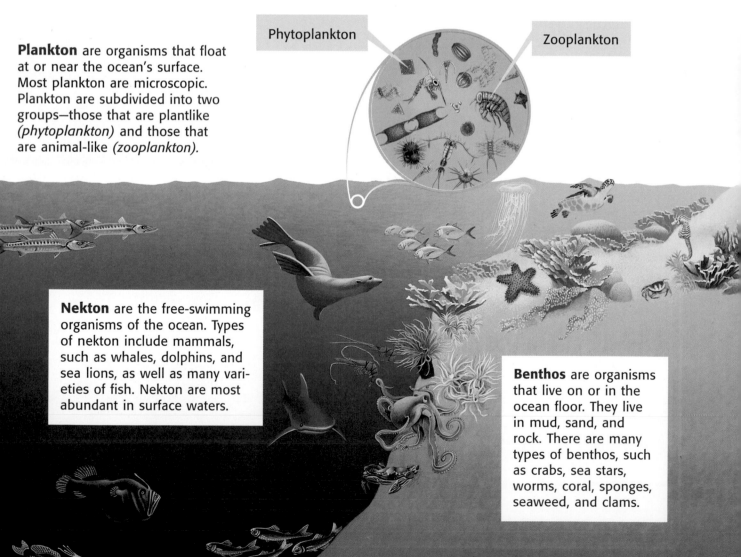

Phytoplankton

Zooplankton

Plankton are organisms that float at or near the ocean's surface. Most plankton are microscopic. Plankton are subdivided into two groups—those that are plantlike *(phytoplankton)* and those that are animal-like *(zooplankton).*

Nekton are the free-swimming organisms of the ocean. Types of nekton include mammals, such as whales, dolphins, and sea lions, as well as many varieties of fish. Nekton are most abundant in surface waters.

Benthos are organisms that live on or in the ocean floor. They live in mud, sand, and rock. There are many types of benthos, such as crabs, sea stars, worms, coral, sponges, seaweed, and clams.

The Benthic Environment

In addition to being divided into zones based on depth, the ocean floor is divided into ecological zones based on where different types of benthos live. These zones are grouped into one major marine environment—the benthic environment. The **benthic environment,** or bottom environment, is the ocean floor and all the organisms that live on or in it.

Intertidal Zone The shallowest benthic zone, the *intertidal zone,* is located between the low-tide and high-tide limits. Twice a day, the intertidal zone transforms. As the tide flows in, the zone is covered with ocean water, and as the tide retreats, the intertidal zone is exposed to the air and sun.

Intertidal organisms must be able to live both underwater and on exposed land. Some organisms attach themselves to rocks and reefs to avoid being washed out to sea during low tide, as shown in **Figure 8.** Clams, oysters, barnacles, and crabs have tough shells that give them protection against strong waves during high tide and against harsh sunlight during low tide. Some animals can burrow in sand or between rocks. Plants such as seaweed have strong *holdfasts* (rootlike structures) that allow them to grow in this zone.

Sublittoral Zone The *sublittoral zone* begins where the intertidal zones ends, at the low-tide limit, and extends to the edge of the continental shelf. This benthic zone is more stable than the intertidal zone; the temperature, water pressure, and amount of sunlight remain fairly constant. Consequently, sublittoral organisms, such as corals, shown in **Figure 9,** do not have to cope with as much change as intertidal organisms. Although the sublittoral zone extends down 200 m below sea level, plants and most animals stay in the upper 100 m, where sunlight reaches the ocean floor.

Biology
CONNECTION

Coral reefs, found in shallow marine waters, have the largest concentration of life in the ocean. Layers of skeletons from animals called *corals* form the reefs, which are the largest animal structures on Earth. Many other organisms live on, around, and even in coral reefs.

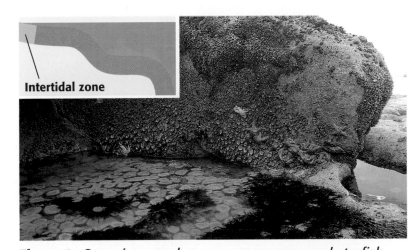

Figure 8 *Organisms such as sea anemones and starfish attach themselves to rocks and reefs. These organisms must be able to survive wet and dry conditions.*

Figure 9 *Corals, like many other types of organisms, can live in both the sublittoral zone and the intertidal zone. However, they are more common in the sublittoral zone.*

Figure 10 *Octopuses are one of the animals common to the bathyal zone.*

Figure 11 *Tube worms can tolerate higher temperatures than most other organisms. These animals survive in water as hot as 81°C.*

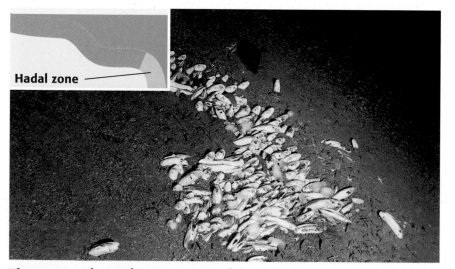

Figure 12 *These clams are one of the few types of organisms known to live in the hadal zone.*

Bathyal Zone The *bathyal zone* extends from the edge of the continental shelf to the abyssal plain. The depth of this zone ranges from 200 m to 4,000 m below sea level. Because of the lack of sunlight at these depths, plant life is scarce in this part of the benthic environment. Animals in this zone include sponges, *brachiopods,* sea stars, *echinoids,* and octopuses, such as the one shown in **Figure 10.**

Abyssal Zone No plants and very few animals live in the *abyssal zone*, which is on the abyssal plain. Among the abyssal animal types are crabs, sponges, worms, and sea cucumbers. Many of these organisms, such as the tube worms shown in **Figure 11,** live around hot-water vents called *black smokers*. The abyssal zone can reach 6,000 m in depth. Scientists know very little about this benthic zone because it is so deep and dark.

Hadal Zone The deepest benthic zone is the *hadal zone*. This zone consists of the floor of the ocean trenches and any organisms found there. Scientists know even less about the hadal zone than they do about the abyssal zone. So far, scientists have discovered a type of sponge, a few species of worms, and a type of clam, which is shown in **Figure 12.**

The Pelagic Environment

The **pelagic environment** is the entire volume of water in the ocean and the marine organisms that live above the ocean floor. There are two major zones in the pelagic environment—the *neritic zone* and the *oceanic zone.*

Neritic Zone The neritic zone includes the volume of water that covers the continental shelf. This warm, shallow zone contains the largest concentration of marine life. This is due to an abundance of sunlight and to the many benthos below the neritic zone that serve as a food supply. Fish, plankton, and marine mammals, such as the one in **Figure 13,** are just a few of the animal groups found here.

Oceanic Zone The oceanic zone includes the volume of water that covers the entire sea floor except for the continental shelf. In the deeper parts of the oceanic zone, the water temperature is colder and the pressure is much greater than in the neritic zone. Also, organisms are more spread out in the oceanic zone than in the neritic zone. While many of the same organisms that live in the neritic zone are found throughout the upper regions, some strange animals lurk in the darker depths, as shown in **Figure 14.** Other animals in the deeper parts of this zone include giant squids and some whale species.

Figure 13 *Many marine mammals, such as this dolphin, live in the neritic zone.*

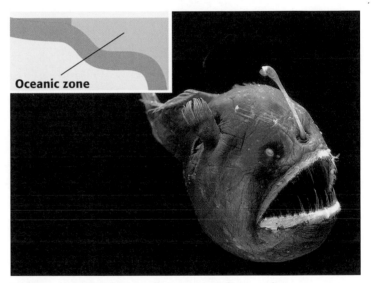

Figure 14 *The anglerfish is a tricky predator that uses a natural lure attached to its head to attract prey.*

SECTION REVIEW

1. List and briefly describe the three main groups of marine organisms.

2. Name the two ocean environments. List the zones of each environment.

3. **Making Predictions** How would the ocean's ecological zones change if sea level dropped 300 m?

internet**connect**

*sci*LINKS
NSTA

TOPIC: Life in Oceans
GO TO: www.scilinks.org
*sci*LINKS NUMBER: HSTE315

Terms to Learn

desalination

What You'll Do

- List two methods of harvesting the ocean's living resources.
- List nonliving resources in the ocean.
- Describe the ocean's energy resources.

Resources from the Ocean

The ocean offers a seemingly endless supply of resources. Food, raw materials, energy, and drinkable water are all harvested from the ocean. And there are probably undiscovered resources in unexplored regions of the ocean. As human populations have grown, however, the demand for these resources has increased while the availability has decreased.

Living Resources

People have been harvesting marine plants and animals for food for thousands of years. Many civilizations formed in coastal regions that were rich enough in marine life to support growing human populations. Read on to learn how humans harvest marine life today.

Fishing the Ocean Harvesting food from the ocean is a multi-billion-dollar industry. Of all the seafood taken from the ocean, fish are the most abundant. Almost 75 million tons of fish are harvested each year. With improved technology, such as sonar and drift nets, fishermen have become better at locating and taking fish from the ocean. **Figure 15** illustrates how drift nets are used. In recent years, many people have become concerned that we are overfishing the ocean—taking more fish than can be naturally replaced. Also, a few years ago, the public became aware that animals other than fish, especially dolphins and turtles, were accidentally being caught in drift nets. Today the fishing industry is making efforts to prevent overfishing and damage to other wildlife from drift nets.

Figure 15 *Drift nets are fishing nets that cover kilometers of ocean. Fishermen can harvest entire schools of fish in one drift net.*

Farming the Ocean As overfishing reduces fish populations and laws regulating fishing become stricter, it is becoming more difficult to supply our demand for fish. To compensate for this, many ocean fish, such as salmon and turbot, are being captively bred in fish farms. Fish farming requires several holding ponds, each containing fish at a certain level of development. **Figure 16** shows a holding pond in a fish farm. When the fish are old enough, they are harvested and packaged for shipping.

Figure 16 *Consuming fish raised in a fish farm helps reduce the number of fish harvested from the ocean.*

Savory Seaweed Fish are not the only seafood harvested in a farmlike setting. Shrimp, oysters, crabs, and mussels are raised in enclosed areas near the shore. Mussels and oysters are grown attached to ropes, as shown in **Figure 17.** Huge nets line the nursery area, preventing the animals from being eaten by their natural predators.

Many species of algae, commonly known as seaweed, are also harvested from the ocean. For example, kelp, a seaweed that grows as much as 33 cm a day, is harvested and used as a thickener in jellies, ice cream, and similar products. The next time you enjoy your favorite ice cream, remember that without seaweed, it would be a runny mess! Seaweed is rich in protein, and several species of seaweed are staples of the Japanese diet. For example, the rolled varieties of sushi, a Japanese dish, are wrapped in seaweed.

Figure 17 *In addition to fish, there are many other types of seafood, such as these mussels, that are raised in farms.*

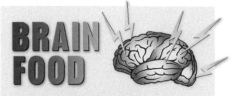
Nonliving Resources

Humans harvest many types of nonliving resources from the ocean. These resources provide raw materials, drinkable water, and energy for our expanding population. Some resources are easily obtained, while others are rare or difficult to harvest.

Oil and Natural Gas Modern civilization continues to be very dependent on oil and natural gas as major sources of energy. Oil and natural gas are *nonrenewable resources,* which means that they are used up faster than they can be replenished naturally. Both oil and natural gas are found under layers of impermeable rock. Petroleum engineers must drill through this rock in order to reach the resources.

Searching for Oil How do petroleum engineers know where to drill for oil and natural gas? Ships with seismic equipment are used for this purpose. Special devices send powerful pulses of sound to the ocean floor. The pulses travel through the water and penetrate the rocks below. The pulses are then reflected back toward the ship, where they are recorded by electronic equipment and analyzed by a computer. The computer readings, such as the one in **Figure 18,** indicate how rock layers are arranged below the ocean floor. Petroleum geologists use these readings to locate a promising area to drill.

Figure 18 *Petroleum geologists look at seismic readings to decide where on the ocean floor to drill for oil and gas.*

Fresh Water and Desalination In some areas of the world where fresh water is limited, people desalinate ocean water. **Desalination** is the process of evaporating sea water so that the water and the salt separate. As the water cools and condenses, it is collected and processed for human use. But desalination is not as simple as it sounds, and it is very costly. Countries with an adequate amount of annual rainfall rely on the fresh water provided by precipitation and therefore do not need costly desalination plants. Some countries located in arid regions of the world must build desalination plants to provide an adequate supply of fresh water. Saudi Arabia, located in the desert region of the Middle East, has one of the largest desalination plants in the world.

Sea-Floor Minerals Mining companies are very interested in mineral nodules that are lying on the ocean floor. These nodules are made mostly of manganese, which can be used to make certain types of steel. They also contain iron, copper, nickel, and cobalt. Other nodules are made of phosphates, which are used in making fertilizer.

Nodules are formed from dissolved substances in sea water that stick to solid objects, such as pebbles. As more substances stick to the coated pebble, a nodule begins to grow. Manganese nodules range from the size of a marble to the size of a soccer ball. The photograph in **Figure 19** shows a number of nodules scattered across the ocean floor. It is believed that 15 percent of the ocean floor is covered with these nodules. However, they are located in the deeper parts of the ocean, and mining them is costly and difficult.

QuickLab

How Much Fresh Water Is There?

1. Fill a large **beaker** with 1,000 mL of **water.** This represents all the water on Earth.

2. Carefully pour 970 mL from the beaker into a **graduated cylinder.** This represents the amount of water in the ocean.

3. Pour another 20 mL from the beaker into a **second graduated cylinder.** This represents the amount of water frozen in icecaps and glaciers.

4. Pour another 5 mL into a **third graduated cylinder.** This represents nonconsumable water on land.

5. Take a look at the leftover water. This represents Earth's supply of fresh water.

Put freshwater problems on ice! Turn to page 67 to find out how.

Figure 19 *These manganese nodules could make you wealthy if you knew an affordable way to mine them.*

Figure 20 Using Tides to Generate Electricity

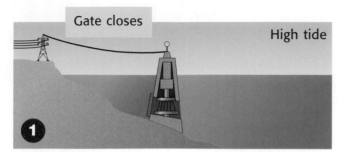

As the tide rises, water enters a bay behind a dam. The gate then closes at high tide.

The gate remains closed as the tide lowers.

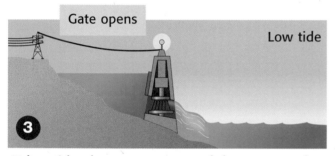

At low tide, the gate opens, and the water rushes through the dam, moving the turbines, which in turn create electricity.

Tidal Energy The ocean creates several types of energy resources simply because of its constant movement. The gravitational pull of the sun and moon causes the ocean to rise and fall as tides. *Tidal energy,* energy generated from the movement of tides, is an excellent alternative source of energy. If the water during high tide can be rushed through a narrow coastal passageway, the water's force can be powerful enough to generate electricity. **Figure 20** shows how this works. Tidal energy is a clean, inexpensive, and renewable resource once the dam is built. A *renewable resource* can be replenished, in time, after being used. Unfortunately, tidal energy is practical only in a few areas of the world, where the coastline has shallow, narrow channels. For example, the coastline at Cook Inlet, in Alaska, is perfect for generating tidal power.

Wave Energy Have you ever stood on the beach and watched as waves crashed onto the shore? This constant motion is an energy resource. Wave energy, like tidal energy, is a clean, renewable resource.

Recently, computer programs have been developed to analyze the energy of waves. Researchers have located certain areas of the world where wave energy can generate enough electricity to make it worthwhile to build power plants. Wave energy in the North Sea is strong enough to produce power for parts of Scotland and England.

internet connect

SCiLINKS
NSTA

TOPIC: Ocean Resources
GO TO: www.scilinks.org
*sci*LINKS NUMBER: HSTE320

SECTION REVIEW

1. List two methods of harvesting the ocean's living resources.

2. Name four nonliving resources in the ocean.

3. **Interpreting Graphics** Take another look at Figure 20. As the tide is rising, will the gate be open or closed? How might this affect the turbines?

Terms to Learn

nonpoint-source pollution

What You'll Do

◆ List different types of ocean pollution.

◆ Explain how to prevent or minimize different types of ocean pollution.

◆ Outline what is being done to control ocean pollution.

Ocean Pollution

Humans have used the ocean for waste disposal for hundreds, if not thousands, of years. This has harmed the organisms that live in the oceans as well as animals that depend on marine organisms. People are also affected by polluted oceans. Fortunately, we are becoming more aware of ocean pollution, and we are learning from our mistakes.

Sources of Ocean Pollution

There are many sources of ocean pollution. Some of these sources are easily identified, but others are more difficult to pinpoint. Read on to find out where different types of ocean pollution come from and how they affect the ocean.

Trash Dumping People dump trash in many places, including the ocean. In the 1980s, scientists became alarmed by the kind of trash that was washing up on beaches. Bandages, vials of blood, and syringes (needles) were found among the waste. Some of the blood in the vials even contained the AIDS virus. The Environmental Protection Agency (EPA) began an investigation and discovered that hospitals in the United States produce an average of 3 million tons of medical waste each year. And where does some of this trash end up? You guessed it—in the ocean. Because of stricter laws, much of this medical waste is now buried in sanitary landfills. However, dumping trash in the deeper part of the ocean is still a common practice in many countries.

Figure 21 *This barge is headed out to the open ocean, where it will dump the trash it carries.*

Saving Our Ocean Resources

Although humans have done much to harm the ocean's resources, we have also begun to do more to save them. From international treaties to volunteer cleanups, efforts to conserve the ocean's resources are making an impact around the world.

Nations Take Notice When ocean pollution reached an all-time high, many countries recognized the need to work together to solve the problem. In 1989, 64 countries ratified a treaty that prohibits the dumping of mercury, cadmium compounds, certain plastics, oil, and high-level radioactive wastes into the ocean. Many other international agreements restricting ocean pollution have been made, but enforcing them is often difficult.

In spite of efforts to protect the ocean, waste dumping and oil spills still occur, and contaminated organisms continue to wash ashore. Why are the laws not working as well as they should? Enforcing these laws takes money and human resources, and many agencies are lacking in both.

Action in the United States The United States, like many other countries, has taken additional measures to control local pollution. In 1972, Congress passed the Clean Water Act, which put the EPA in charge of issuing permits for any dumping of trash into the ocean. Later that year, a stricter law was passed. The U.S. Marine Protection, Research, and Sanctuaries Act prohibits the dumping of any material that would affect human health or welfare, the marine environment or ecosystems, or businesses that depend on the ocean.

Why worry about a few drops of oil? You might be surprised that a little goes a long way. Turn to page 104 in the LabBook to learn more.

Ocean Treaty

Get together with your classmates and divide yourselves into three groups: Nation A, Nation B, and Nation C. All three nations are located near the ocean, and all three nations share borders. Nation A has a very rich supply of oil, which it transports around the world. Nation B currently depends on nuclear energy and has many nuclear power plants near its shores. Nation B has no place on land to store radioactive waste from its nuclear power plants. Nation C sells nuclear technology to Nation B, buys oil from Nation A, and has the world's most diverse coastal ecosystem. The three nations must form a treaty to safeguard against ocean pollution without seriously harming any of their economies. Can you do it?

Figure 25 *The Adopt-a-Beach program in Texas has been a huge success.*

Citizens Take Charge Citizens of many countries have demanded that their governments do more to solve the growing problem of ocean pollution. Because of public outcry, the United States now spends more than $130 million each year monitoring the oceans. United States citizens have also begun to take the matter into their own hands. In the early 1980s, citizens began organizing beach cleanups. One of the largest cleanups is the semiannual Adopt-a-Beach program, shown in **Figure 25,** that originated with the Texas Coastal Cleanup campaign. Millions of tons of trash have been gathered from the beaches, and people are being educated about the hazards of ocean dumping.

Though governments pass laws against ocean dumping, keeping the oceans clean is everyone's responsibility. The next time you and your family visit the beach, make sure the only items you leave behind on the sand are hermit crabs, shells, and maybe a few sand dollars.

SECTION REVIEW

1. List three types of ocean pollution. How can each of these types be prevented or minimized?

2. Which type of ocean pollution is most common?

3. **Summarizing Data** List and describe three measures that governments have taken to control ocean pollution.

internet connect

sci LINKS.
NSTA

TOPIC: Ocean Pollution
GO TO: www.scilinks.org
***sci*LINKS NUMBER:** HSTE323

Making Models Lab

Probing the Depths

In the 1870s, the crew of the ship the HMS *Challenger* used a wire and a weight to discover and map some of the deepest places in the world's oceans. The crew members tied a wire to a weight and dropped the weight overboard. When the weight reached the bottom of the ocean, they hauled the weight back up to the surface and measured the length of the wet wire. In this way, they were eventually able to map the ocean floor. In this activity, you will model this method of mapping by making a map of an ocean-floor model.

MATERIALS

- modeling clay
- shoe box and lid
- scissors
- 8 unsharpened pencils
- metric ruler

Procedure

1. Use the clay to make a model ocean floor in the shoe box. Give the floor some mountains and valleys.

2. Cut eight holes in a line along the center of the lid. The holes should be just big enough to slide a pencil through. Close the box.

3. Exchange boxes with another student or group of students. Do not look into the box.

4. Copy the table on the next page into your ScienceLog. Also make a copy of the graph on the next page.

5. Measure the length of the probe (pencil) in centimeters. Record the length in your data table.

6. Gently insert the probe into the first hole position in the box until it touches the bottom. Do not push the probe down; pushing it down could affect your reading.

7. Making sure the probe is straight up and down, measure the length of probe showing above the lid. Record your data in the data table.

8. Use the following formula to calculate the depth in centimeters:

$$\left(\begin{array}{c}\textit{original length} \\ \textit{of probe}\end{array}\right) - \left(\begin{array}{c}\textit{amount of} \\ \textit{probe showing}\end{array}\right) = \textit{depth in cm}$$

Ocean Depth Chart

Hole position	Original length of probe (cm)	Amount of probe showing (cm)	Depth in centimeters	Depth in meters (cm × 200)
1				
2				
3				
4				
5				
6				
7				
8				

DO NOT WRITE IN BOOK

9 Use the scale 1 cm = 200 m to convert the depth in centimeters to meters to better represent real ocean depths. Add the data to your table.

10 Transfer the data to your graph for position 1.

11 Repeat steps 5–10 for the additional positions in the box.

12 After plotting all the points on your graph, connect the points with a smooth curve.

13 Put a pencil in each of the holes in the shoe box. Compare the rise and fall of the set of pencils with your graph.

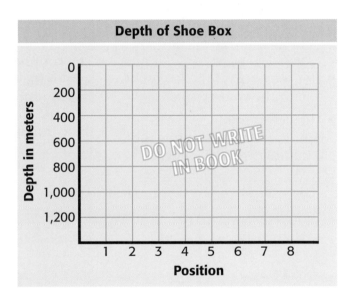

Analysis

14 How deep was your deepest point? your shallowest point?

15 Did your graph resemble the ocean-floor model, as shown by the pencils? If not, why not?

16 What difficulties might scientists have when measuring the real ocean floor? Do they ever get to "open the box"? Explain your answer.

Chapter Highlights

Vocabulary

salinity *(p. 36)*

thermocline *(p. 37)*

water cycle *(p. 39)*

Section Notes

- The four oceans as we know them today formed within the last 300 million years.

- Salts have been added to the ocean for billions of years.

- The three temperature zones of ocean water are the surface zone, thermocline, and deep zone.

- The ocean plays the largest role in the water cycle.

- The ocean stabilizes Earth's conditions by absorbing and retaining thermal energy.

Vocabulary

continental shelf *(p. 42)*

continental slope *(p. 42)*

continental rise *(p. 42)*

abyssal plain *(p. 42)*

mid-ocean ridge *(p. 43)*

rift valley *(p. 43)*

seamount *(p. 43)*

ocean trench *(p. 43)*

Section Notes

- The ocean floor is divided into zones based on depth and slope.

- The continental margin consists of the continental shelf, the continental slope, and the continental rise.

- The deep-ocean basin consists of the abyssal plain, with features such as mid-ocean ridges, rift valleys, seamounts, and ocean trenches.

- In addition to directly studying the ocean floor, scientists indirectly study the ocean floor using sonar and satellites.

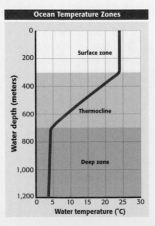

☑ Skills Check

Math Concepts

PERCENTAGES Percentages are a way of describing the parts within a whole. Percentages are expressed in hundredths. Take another look at Figure 1 on page 36. The pie chart shows the percentages of dissolved solids in ocean water. The amount of chlorine (Cl) dissolved in the ocean is 55 percent. This means that 55 of every 100 parts of dissolved solids in the ocean are chlorine.

Visual Understanding

TEMPERATURE ZONES Look back at the line graph on page 37 to review why the temperature of the ocean decreases with increasing depth.

SECTION 3

Vocabulary

plankton *(p. 46)*

nekton *(p. 46)*

benthos *(p. 46)*

benthic environment *(p. 47)*

pelagic environment *(p. 49)*

Section Notes

- There are three main groups of marine life—plankton, nekton, and benthos.

- The two main ocean environments—the benthic and pelagic environments—are divided into ecological zones based on the locations of organisms that live in the environments.

SECTION 4

Vocabulary

desalination *(p. 53)*

Section Notes

- Humans depend on the ocean for living and non-living resources.

- Ocean farms raise fish and other marine life to help feed growing human populations.

- Nonliving ocean resources include oil and natural gas, fresh water, minerals, and tidal and wave energy.

SECTION 5

Vocabulary

nonpoint-source pollution *(p. 56)*

Section Notes

- Types of ocean pollution include trash dumping, sludge dumping, nonpoint-source pollution, and oil spills.

- Nonpoint-source pollution cannot be traced to specific points of origin.

- Efforts to save ocean resources include international treaties and volunteer cleanups.

Labs

Investigating an Oil Spill *(p. 104)*

---

 internetconnect

GO TO: go.hrw.com

Visit the **HRW** Web site for a variety of learning tools related to this chapter. Just type in the keyword:

KEYWORD: HSTOCE

 **N S T A** **GO TO:** www.scilinks.org

Visit the **National Science Teachers Association** on-line Web site for Internet resources related to this chapter. Just type in the *sci*LINKS number for more information about the topic:

TOPIC: Exploring Earth's Oceans	*sci*LINKS NUMBER: HSTE305
TOPIC: The Ocean Floor	*sci*LINKS NUMBER: HSTE310
TOPIC: Life in the Oceans	*sci*LINKS NUMBER: HSTE315
TOPIC: Ocean Resources	*sci*LINKS NUMBER: HSTE320
TOPIC: Ocean Pollution	*sci*LINKS NUMBER: HSTE323

Chapter Review

To complete the following sentences, choose the correct term from each pair of terms listed below:

1. The region of the ocean floor that is closest to the shoreline is the __?__. (*continental shelf* or *continental slope*)

2. Below the surface layer of the ocean is a layer of water that gets colder with depth and extends to a depth of 700 m. This layer is called the __?__. (*thermocline* or *benthic environment*)

3. __?__ typically float at or near the ocean's surface. (*Plankton* or *Nekton*)

Correct the wrong terminology in each of the following sentences. A word bank is provided.

4. The water cycle is the process of evaporating sea water so that the water and salt separate.

5. Types of nekton include sea stars and clams.

Word bank:
nonpoint-source pollution, plankton, desalination, benthos

Explain the difference between the words in each of the following pairs:

6. ocean trench/rift valley

7. salinity/desalination

8. nekton/benthos

9. pelagic environment/benthic environment

Multiple Choice

10. The largest ocean is the
    a. Indian Ocean. c. Atlantic Ocean.
    b. Pacific Ocean. d. Arctic Ocean.

11. One of the most abundant elements in the ocean is
    a. potassium. c. chlorine.
    b. calcium. d. magnesium.

12. Which of the following affects the ocean's salinity?
    a. fresh water added by rivers
    b. currents
    c. evaporation
    d. all of the above

13. Most precipitation falls
    a. on land.
    b. into lakes and rivers.
    c. into the ocean.
    d. in rain forests.

14. Which benthic zone has a depth range between 200 m and 4,000 m?
    a. bathyal zone c. hadal zone
    b. abyssal zone d. sublittoral zone

15. The ocean floor and all the organisms that live on it or in it is the
    a. benthic environment.
    b. pelagic environment.
    c. neritic zone.
    d. oceanic zone.

Short Answer

16. Why does coastal water in areas with hotter, drier climates typically have a higher salinity than coastal water in cooler, more humid areas?

17. What is the difference between the abyssal plain and the abyssal zone?

18. How do the continental shelf, the continental slope, the continental rise, and the continental margin relate to each other?

Concept Mapping

19. Use the following term to create a concept map: marine life, plankton, nekton, benthos, benthic environment, pelagic environment.

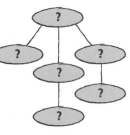

CRITICAL THINKING AND PROBLEM SOLVING

Write one or two sentences to answer the following questions:

20. Other than obtaining fresh water, what benefit comes from desalination?

21. Explain the difference between a bathymetric profile and a seismic reading.

MATH IN SCIENCE

22. Imagine that you are in the kelp-farming business and that your kelp grows 33 cm per day. You begin harvesting when your plants are 50 cm tall. During the first seven days of harvest, you cut 10 cm off the top of your kelp plants each day. How tall would your kelp plants be after the seventh day of harvesting?

INTERPRETING GRAPHICS

Examine the image below, and answer the questions that follow:

Ecological Zones of the Ocean

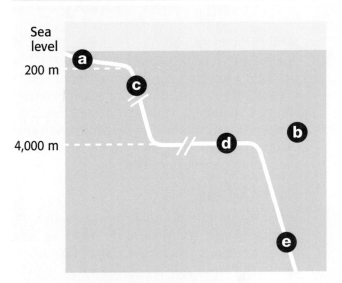

23. At which point (a, b, c, d, or e) would you most likely find an anglerfish?

24. At which point would you most likely find tube worms?

25. Which ecological zone is at point c? Which depth zone is at point c?

26. Name a type of organism you might find at point e.

Reading Check-up

Take a minute to review your answers to the Pre-Reading Questions found at the bottom of page 32. Have your answers changed? If necessary, revise your answers based on what you have learned since you began this chapter.

Exploring Ocean Life

Jacques Cousteau, born in France in 1910, opened the eyes of countless people to the sea. During his long life, Cousteau explored Earth's oceans and documented the amazing variety of life they contained. Jacques Cousteau was an explorer, environmentalist, inventor, and teacher who inspired millions with his joy and wonder at the watery part of our planet.

Early Dives

Cousteau performed his first underwater diving mission at age 10. At summer camp he was asked to collect trash from the camp's lake. The young Cousteau quickly realized that working underwater without goggles or breathing equipment was a tremendous challenge.

Cousteau had another early underwater experience when he visited Southeast Asia. He saw people diving into the water to catch fish with their bare hands. This fascinated Cousteau. Even at a young age, he was thinking about how to make equipment that would let a person breathe underwater.

▲ *Cousteau in front of the* Calypso II

Underwater Flight

As a young man, Cousteau and some friends developed the aqualung, a self-contained breathing system for underwater exploration. As someone who had often dreamed of flying, Cousteau was thrilled with his invention. After one of his first dives, Cousteau explained, "I experimented with all possible maneuvers— loops, somersaults, and barrel rolls. . . . Delivered from gravity and buoyancy, I flew around in space."

Using the aqualung and other underwater equipment he developed, Cousteau began making underwater films. In 1950, he bought a boat named *Calypso,* which became his home and floating laboratory. For the next 40 years, through his films and television series, Cousteau brought what he called "the silent world" of the oceans and seas to living rooms everywhere.

A Protector of Life

Cousteau was long an outspoken defender of the environment. "When I saw all this beauty under the sea, I fell in love with it. And finally, when I realized to what extent the oceans were threatened, I decided to campaign as vigorously as I could against everything that threatened what I loved."

Jacques Cousteau died in 1997 at age 87. Before his death, he dedicated the *Calypso II,* a new research vessel, to the children of the world.

Write About It

▶ Ocean pollution and overfishing are subjects of intense debate. Think about these issues, and discuss them with your classmates. Then write an essay in which you try to convince readers of your point of view.

EYE ON THE ENVIRONMENT

Putting Freshwater Problems on Ice

Imagine how different your life would be if you couldn't get fresh water. What would you drink? How would you clean things? The Earth has enough fresh water to supply 100 billion liters to each person, yet water shortages affect millions of people every day. So what's the problem?

The Ice-Water Planet

Three-quarters of Earth's fresh water is frozen in polar icecaps. Plenty of fresh water is there, but people can't use water that is frozen and thousands of kilometers away.

The ice sheet that covers Antarctica is thousands of meters thick and is almost twice the size of the United States. Hundreds of huge chunks break off its edges every year. These icebergs, which are made up entirely of frozen fresh water, float away into the sea and eventually melt. Water from 1 year's worth of these icebergs would be enough to supply all of southern California for more than a century. So why not use it?

Obvious but Not Easy

Transporting icebergs to areas that need fresh water is harder than it sounds. For one thing, many of the icebergs are huge. The largest ever recorded was about the size of Connecticut. Even small icebergs may be 2 km long and 1 km wide.

Researchers have considered many methods of transporting icebergs. Most of the ideas involve pushing or towing icebergs through the water. A few ideas involve attaching engines and propellers directly to the icebergs.

However, because icebergs are so large, it takes a long time to move them. And when an iceberg finally does get somewhere, a considerable amount of it has melted. To prevent melting, insulating materials could be wrapped around an iceberg.

▲ *Icebergs such as this one might provide water in the future.*

A Worthy Investment

Lakes and ground water still provide the cheapest fresh water in most areas. However, if there is no lake, river, or well water available, icebergs may then be a reasonable option to consider. Even though transporting icebergs is difficult, it may still be worthwhile to try. Irrigating 100 km^2 of desert with water from icebergs might cost as much as $1 million, but purifying enough sea water to irrigate that amount of desert could cost over $1 billion.

People in arid regions have spent considerable time on iceberg research. So far, no one has set up a program for harvesting icebergs. But someday water from icebergs may flow from our household faucets.

An Icy Investigation

▶ Float an ice cube in a bowl of cold water, and record the time it takes the cube to melt. Then try to insulate other ice cubes with different materials, such as cloth, plastic wrap, and aluminum foil. Which material works best? How could this material be used on real icebergs?

CHAPTER

3

The Movement of Ocean Water

Sections

Pre-Reading Questions

1. What factors control ocean currents?

2. What causes the ocean tides?

An Ocean Stream

The Gulf Stream current carries warm tropical water from the Caribbean Sea all the way to the North Atlantic Ocean. The climate in the British Isles, where the current ends, is controlled by the current's warm waters, which make the isles much warmer than other countries nearby. In this chapter, you will learn how currents like the Gulf Stream are formed. You also will learn about the other ways that ocean water moves and how these movements affect our lives.

WHEN *WHIRLS* COLLIDE

Ocean currents in the Northern Hemisphere flow in a clockwise direction, while currents in the Southern Hemisphere flow in a counterclockwise direction. Sometimes, southern currents flow across the equator into the Northern Hemisphere and begin flowing clockwise. Do this activity to find out how currents flowing in opposite directions affect one another.

Procedure

1. Fill a large **tub** with **water** 5 cm deep.

2. Add **10 drops of red food coloring** to the water on one end of the tub.

3. Add **10 drops of blue food coloring** to the water at the other end of the tub.

4. Using a **pencil,** quickly stir the water at one end of the tub in a clockwise direction while your partner stirs the water at the other end in a counterclockwise direction. Stir both ends for about 5 seconds.

5. In your ScienceLog, draw what you see happening in the tub immediately after you stop stirring. (Both ends should still be swirling.)

Analysis

6. How did the blue water and the red water interact?

7. How does this activity relate to the ocean currents in the Northern and Southern Hemispheres?

What You'll Do

◆ Describe surface currents, and list the three factors that control them.
◆ Describe deep currents.
◆ Illustrate the factors involved in deep-current movement.
◆ Explain how currents affect climate.

Currents

Imagine that you are stranded on a desert island. You stuff a distress message into a bottle and throw it into the ocean, hoping it will find its way to someone who will send help. Is there any way to predict where your bottle may land?

One Way to Explore Currents

In the 1940s, a Norwegian explorer named Thor Heyerdahl tried to answer similar questions that involved human migration across the ocean. Heyerdahl theorized that the inhabitants of Polynesia originally sailed from Peru on rafts powered only by the wind and ocean currents. Unable to convince scientists of his theory, he decided to prove it. In 1947, Heyerdahl and a crew of five people set sail from Peru on a raft, as shown in **Figure 1.**

Figure 1 *The handcrafted* Kon-Tiki *was made mainly from materials that would have been available to ancient Peruvians.*

On the 97th day of their expedition, Heyerdahl and his crew landed on an island in Polynesia. Currents had carried the raft westward more than 6,000 km across the South Pacific. This supported Heyerdahl's theory that ocean currents carried the ancient Peruvians across the Pacific to Polynesia. Now let's take a closer look at currents. For example, what determines the direction in which a current moves? What forces create a current? Read on to learn the answers to these and other questions about currents.

Surface Currents

Streamlike movements of water that occur at or near the surface of the ocean are called **surface currents.** Some surface currents are several thousand kilometers in length, traveling across entire oceans. The Gulf Stream, which is one of the longest surface currents, transports 25 times more water than all the rivers in the world. Surface currents are controlled by three factors: global winds, the Coriolis effect, and continental deflections. These three factors keep surface currents flowing in distinct patterns around the Earth.

Global Winds Have you ever blown gently on a cup of hot chocolate? You may have noticed ripples moving across the surface. These ripples are caused by a tiny surface current created by your breath. In much the same way, winds blowing across the Earth's surface create surface currents in the ocean. Surface currents can reach depths of several hundred meters and lengths of several thousand kilometers.

Different winds cause currents to flow in different directions. Near the equator, the winds blow ocean water east to west, but closer to the poles, ocean water is blown west to east, as shown in **Figure 2.** Merchant ships often use these currents to travel more quickly back and forth across the oceans.

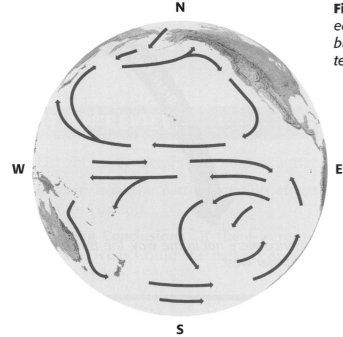

Figure 2 *Surface currents near the equator generally flow from east to west, but surface currents closer to the poles tend to flow from west to east.*

Self-Check

Take another look at Figure 2. As Heyerdahl made his journey in 1947, from what direction would he have noticed the wind blowing? *(See page 136 to check your answer.)*

Deep Currents

Deep currents are streamlike movements of ocean water far below the surface. Unlike surface currents, deep currents are not directly controlled by wind or the Coriolis effect. Instead, they form in parts of the ocean where water density increases. *Density* is the ratio of the mass of a substance to its volume. Two main factors—temperature and salinity—combine to affect the density of ocean water, as shown below. As you can see, both decreasing the temperature of ocean water and increasing the water's salinity increase the water's density.

How Deep Currents Form

Decreasing Temperature In Earth's polar regions, cold air chills the water molecules at the ocean's surface, causing them to slow down and move closer together. This decreases the water's volume, making the water denser. The dense water sinks and eventually travels toward the equator as a deep current along the ocean floor.

Increasing Salinity Through Freezing *Salinity* is a measure of the amount of dissolved solids in a liquid. If the ocean water freezes at the surface, ice will float on top of water because ice is less dense than liquid water. The dissolved solids are squeezed out of the ice and enter the liquid water below the ice, increasing the salinity. Because this water contains more dissolved solids, its density also increases.

Increasing Salinity Through Evaporation Another way salinity increases is through evaporation of surface water, which removes water but leaves solids behind. This is especially common in warm climates. Increasing salinity through freezing or evaporation causes water to become denser and sink to the ocean floor, becoming a deep current.

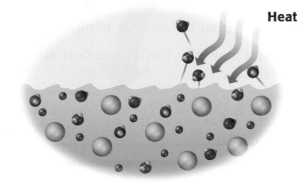

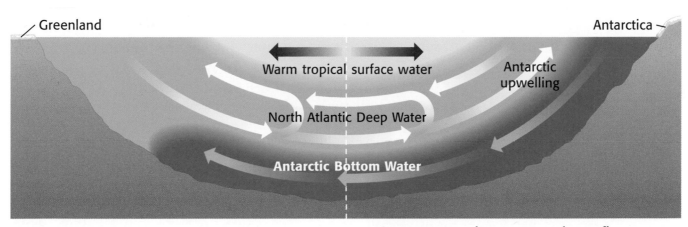

Greenland

Antarctica

Warm tropical surface water

Antarctic upwelling

North Atlantic Deep Water

Antarctic Bottom Water

Figure 6 *Less-dense water always flows on top of denser water, as shown in this cross section.*

Movement of Deep Currents The movement of deep currents as they travel along the ocean floor is very complex. Differences in temperature and salinity, and therefore in density, cause variations in deep currents. For example, the deepest current, the Antarctic Bottom Water, is denser than the North Atlantic Deep Water. Both currents spread out across the ocean floor as they flow toward the same equatorial region. But when the currents meet, the North Atlantic Deep Water actually flows on top of the denser Antarctic Bottom Water, as shown in **Figure 6.** The Antarctic Bottom Water is so dense that it moves incredibly slowly—it takes 750 years for water in this current to make it from Antarctica's coastal waters to the equator!

Currents Trading Places Now that you understand how deep currents form and how they move along the ocean floor, you can learn how they trade places with surface currents. To see how this works, study **Figure 7.**

Figure 7 *This cross section shows the movement of warm water and cold water between polar and equatorial regions.*

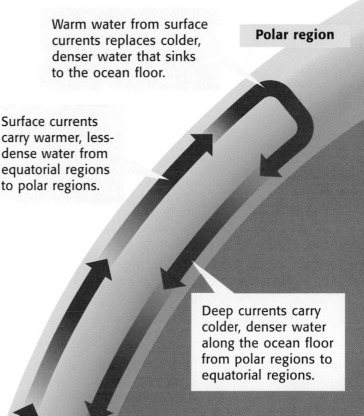

Warm water from surface currents replaces colder, denser water that sinks to the ocean floor.

Polar region

Surface currents carry warmer, less-dense water from equatorial regions to polar regions.

Deep currents carry colder, denser water along the ocean floor from polar regions to equatorial regions.

Water from deep currents rises to replace water leaving in surface currents.

Equatorial region

Surface Currents and Climate

Surface currents greatly affect the climate in many parts of the world. Some surface currents warm or cool coastal areas year-round. Other surface currents sometimes change their circulation pattern. This causes changes in the atmosphere that disrupt the climate in many parts of the world.

Currents That Stabilize Climate Although surface currents are generally much warmer than deep currents, their temperatures do vary. Surface currents are classified as warm-water currents or cold-water currents. Look back at Figure 5 to see where each type is located. Because they are warm or cold, surface currents affect the climate of the land near the area where they flow. For example, warm-water currents create warmer climates in coastal areas that would otherwise be much cooler. Likewise, cold-water currents create cooler climates in coastal areas that would otherwise be much warmer. **Figure 8** shows how a warm-water current and a cold-water current affect coastal climates.

Figure 8 *Warm-water currents, such as the Gulf Stream (top), and cold-water currents, such as the California Current (bottom), can affect the climate of coastal regions.*

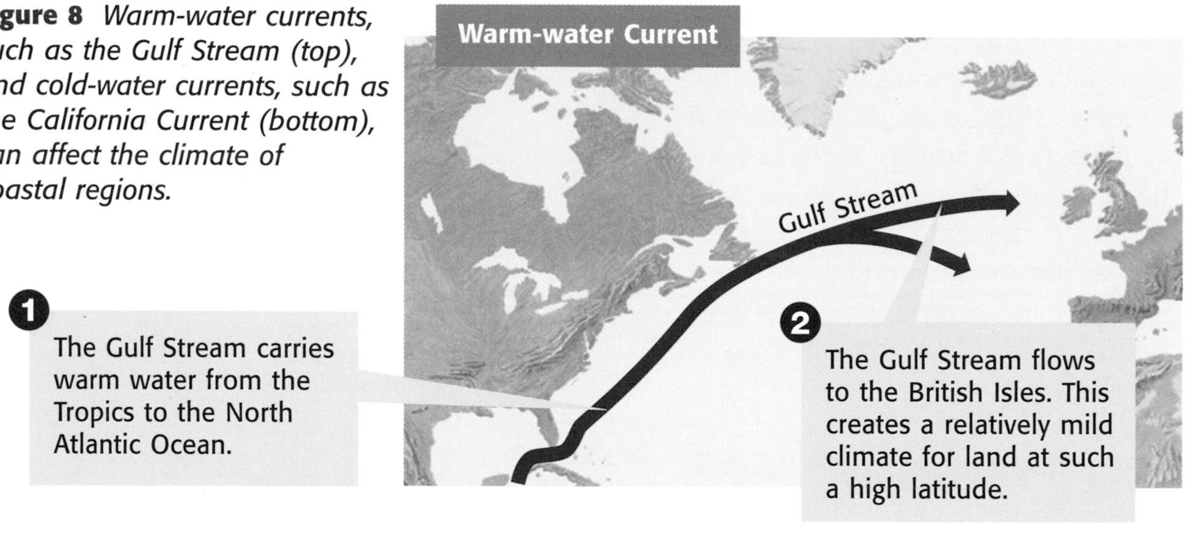

Warm-water Current

Gulf Stream

1 The Gulf Stream carries warm water from the Tropics to the North Atlantic Ocean.

2 The Gulf Stream flows to the British Isles. This creates a relatively mild climate for land at such a high latitude.

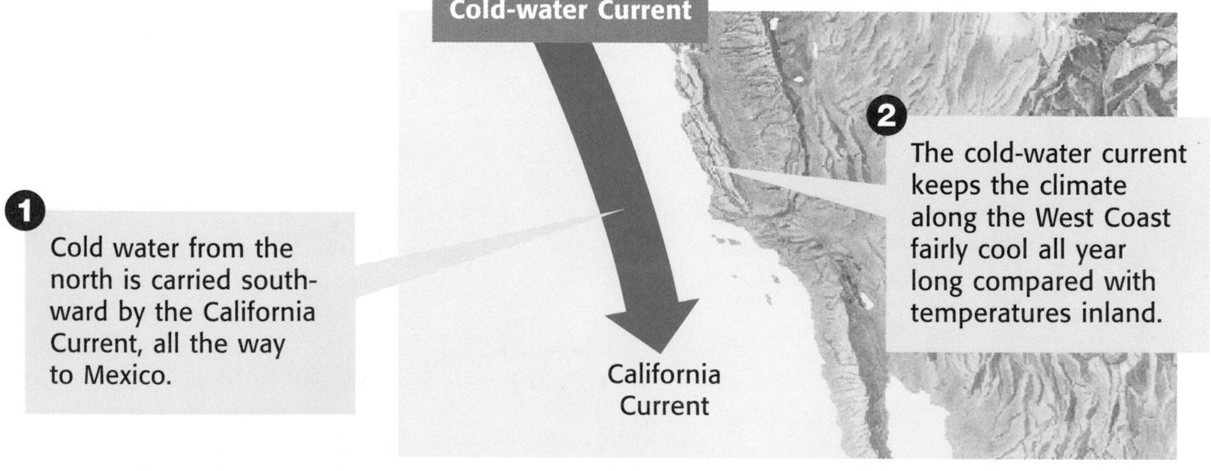

Cold-water Current

1 Cold water from the north is carried southward by the California Current, all the way to Mexico.

2 The cold-water current keeps the climate along the West Coast fairly cool all year long compared with temperatures inland.

California Current

Current Variations—El Niño The surface currents in the tropical region of the Pacific Ocean usually travel with the trade winds from east to west. This builds up warm water in the western Pacific and causes upwelling in the eastern Pacific. **Upwelling** is a process in which cold, nutrient-rich water from the deep ocean rises to the surface and replaces warm surface water. The warm water is blown out to sea by prevailing winds. But every 2 to 12 years, the South Pacific trade winds move less warm water to the western Pacific. As a result, surface water temperatures along the coast of South America rise. Gradually, this warming spreads westward. This periodic change in the location of warm and cool surface waters in the Pacific Ocean is called **El Niño.** El Niño not only affects surface waters but also changes the interaction between the ocean and the atmosphere, resulting in changes in global weather patterns.

BRAIN FOOD

El Niño means "The Child" in Spanish. The term originally referred to a warm current that arrived each year during the Christmas season off the coast of Ecuador and Peru.

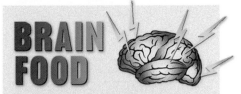

Effects of El Niño El Niño alters weather patterns enough to cause disasters, such as flash floods and mudslides in areas of the world that normally receive little rain. **Figure 9** shows homes destroyed by a mudslide in Southern California. While some regions flood, regions that usually get a lot of rain may experience droughts, which can lead to crop failures.

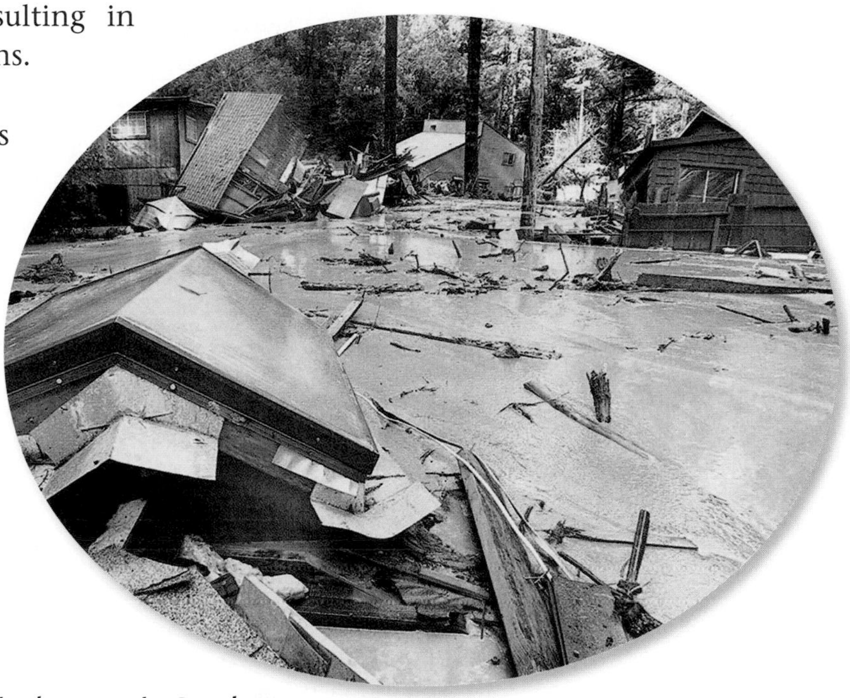

Figure 9 *This damage in Southern California was the result of excessive rain caused by El Niño in 1997.*

SECTION REVIEW

1. How do temperature and salinity relate to deep-current movement?
2. Why is the climate in Scotland relatively mild even though the country is located at a high latitude?
3. **Applying Concepts** Many marine organisms depend on upwelling to bring nutrients to the surface. How might an El Niño affect Peruvians' way of life?

internet**connect**

SCI*LINKS* NSTA

TOPIC: El Niño
GO TO: www.scilinks.org
***sci*LINKS NUMBER:** HSTE335

Terms to Learn

crest	surf
trough	whitecap
wavelength	swells
wave height	tsunami
wave period	storm surge
breaker	

What You'll Do

- ◆ Identify wave components, and explain how they relate to wave movement.
- ◆ Describe how ocean waves form and how they move.
- ◆ Classify types of waves.
- ◆ Analyze types of dangerous waves.

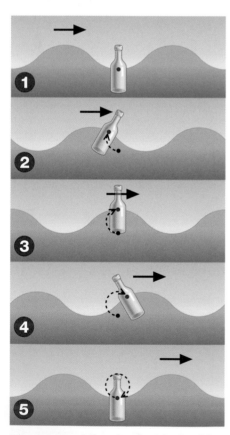

Figure 10 *Like the bottle in this figure, water remains in the same place as waves travel through it.*

Waves

We all know what ocean waves look like. Even if you've never been to the seashore, you've most likely seen waves on television. But what are ocean waves? How do they form and move? Are all waves the same? And what do they do besides drop shells and sand dollars on the beach? Let us examine ocean waves so that we can answer these questions.

Anatomy of a Wave

Waves are made up of two main components—crests and troughs. A **crest** is the highest point of a wave, and a **trough** is the lowest point. Imagine a thrilling roller coaster designed with many rises and dips. The top of a rise on a roller-coaster track is similar to

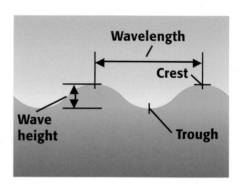

the crest of a wave, and the bottom of a dip in the track resembles the trough of a wave. The distance between two adjacent wave crests or wave troughs is a **wavelength.** The vertical distance between a wave's crest and its trough is a **wave height.**

Wave Formation and Movement

If you have watched ocean waves before, you may have noticed that water appears to move across the ocean's surface. However, this movement is only an illusion. Most waves form as wind blows across the water's surface, transferring energy to the water. As the energy moves through the water, so do the waves. But the water itself stays behind, rising and falling in circular movements. Notice in **Figure 10** that the floating bottle remains in the same spot as the waves travel from left to right. The circle of moving water that the bottle moves with has a diameter that is equal to the height of the waves that created it. Underneath this circle are smaller circles of moving water. The diameters of these circles get smaller with depth because wave energy decreases with depth. Wave energy only reaches to a certain depth. Below that depth, the water is not affected by wave energy.

Specifics of Wave Movement

Waves not only come in different sizes but also travel at different speeds. To calculate wave speed, scientists must know the wavelength and the wave period. **Wave period** is the time between the passage of two wave crests (or troughs) at a fixed point, as shown in **Figure 11.** Dividing wavelength by wave period gives you wave speed, as shown below.

$$\frac{\text{wavelength (m)}}{\text{wave period (s)}} = \text{wave speed (m/s)}$$

For any given wavelength, an increase in the wave period will decrease the wave speed, and a decrease in the wave period will increase the wave speed.

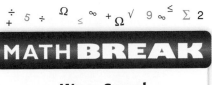

MATH BREAK

Wave Speed

Imagine you are in a rowboat on the open ocean. You count 2 waves traveling right under your boat in 10 seconds. You estimate the wavelength to be 3 m. What is the wave speed?

Figure 11 *The illustration below shows how the wave period is determined.*

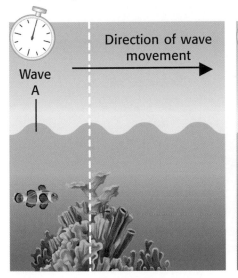

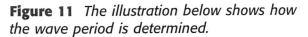

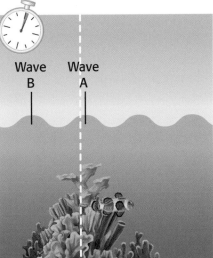

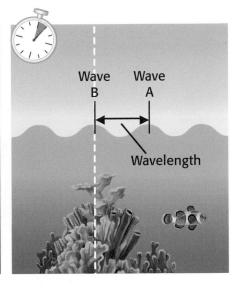

 Notice that the waves are moving from left to right.

❷ *The clock begins running as Wave A passes the reef's peak.*

❸ *The clock stops as Wave B passes the reef's peak. The time shown on the clock (5 seconds) represents the wave period.*

Types of Waves

As you learned earlier in this section, wind forms most ocean waves. However, waves can form by other mechanisms. Underwater earthquakes and landslides as well as impacts by cosmic bodies can form different types of waves. The sizes of the different types of waves can vary, but most move the same way. Depending on their size and the angle at which they hit the shore, waves can generate a variety of near-shore events, some of which can be dangerous to humans.

Deep-Water Waves and Shallow-Water Waves Have you ever wondered why waves increase in height as they approach the shore? The answer has to do with the depth of the water. *Deep-water waves* are waves that move in water that is deeper than one-half of their wavelength. When the waves reach water that is shallower than one-half of their wavelength, they begin to interact with the ocean floor. These waves are called *shallow-water waves*. **Figure 12** shows how deep-water waves become shallow-water waves as they move toward the shore.

As deep-water waves become shallow-water waves, the water particles slow down and build up. This forces more water between wave crests and increases wave height. Gravity eventually pulls the high wave crests down, causing them to crash into the ocean floor as **breakers.** The area where waves first begin to tumble downward, or break, is called the *breaker zone.* Waves continue to break as they move from the breaker zone to the shore. The area between the breaker zone and the shore is called the **surf.**

Figure 12 *Deep-water waves become shallow-water waves when they reach depths of less than half of their wavelength.*

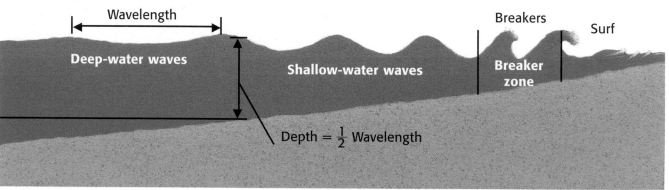

When waves crash on the beach head-on, the water they moved through flows back to the ocean underneath new incoming waves. This movement of water, which carries sand, rock particles, and plankton away from the shore, is called an *undertow*. **Figure 13** illustrates the back-and-forth movement of water at the shore.

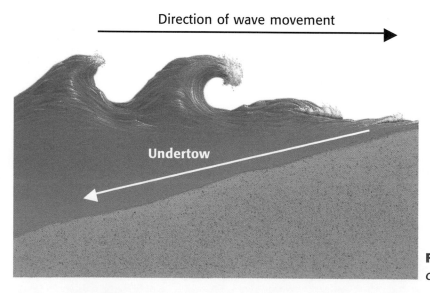

Figure 13 *Head-on waves create an undertow.*

When waves hit the shore at an angle, they cause water to move along the shore in a current called a *longshore current*. This process is shown in **Figure 14.** Longshore currents are responsible for most sediment transport in beach environments. This movement of sand and other sediment both tears down and builds up the coastline. Unfortunately, longshore currents also carry trash and other types of ocean pollution, spreading it along the shore.

Open-Ocean Waves Sometimes waves called whitecaps form in the open ocean. **Whitecaps** are white, foaming waves with very steep crests that break in the open ocean before the waves get close to the shore. These waves usually form during stormy weather, and they are usually short-lived. Calmer winds form waves called swells. **Swells** are rolling waves that move in a steady procession across the ocean. Swells have longer wavelengths than whitecaps and can travel for thousands of kilometers. **Figure 15** shows how whitecaps and swells differ.

Figure 14 *Longshore currents form where waves approach beaches at an angle.*

Figure 15 *Whitecaps, shown in the photo at left, break in the open ocean, while swells, shown in the photo at right, roll gently in the open ocean.*

QuickLab

Do the Wave

1. Tie one end of a thin piece of **rope** to a doorknob.

2. Tie a **ribbon** around the rope halfway between the doorknob and the other end of the rope.

3. Holding the rope at the untied end, quickly move the rope up and down, and observe the ribbon.

4. How does the movement of the rope and ribbon relate to the movement of water and deep-water waves?

5. Repeat step 3, but move the rope higher and lower this time.

6. How does this affect the waves in the rope?

TRY at HOME

Tsunamis Professional surfers often travel to Hawaii to catch some of the highest waves in the world. But even the best surfers would not be able to handle a tsunami. **Tsunamis** are waves that form when a large volume of ocean water is suddenly moved up or down. This movement can be caused by underwater earthquakes, volcanic eruptions, landslides, underwater explosions, or the impact of a meteorite or comet. The majority of tsunamis occur in the Pacific Ocean because of the greater number of earthquakes in that region. **Figure 16** shows how an earthquake can generate a tsunami.

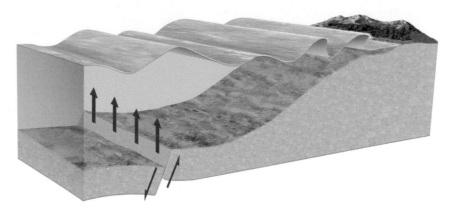

Figure 16 *An upward shift in the ocean floor creates an earthquake. The energy released by the earthquake pushes a large volume of water upward, creating a series of tsunamis.*

When tsunamis near continents, they slow down and their wavelengths shorten as they interact with the ocean floor. As tsunamis get closer together, their wave height increases. Tsunamis can reach more than 30 m in height as they slam into the coast, destroying just about everything in their path. The powerful undertow created by a tsunami can be as destructive as the tsunami itself. **Figure 17** shows a coastal community devastated by a tsunami.

Figure 17 *Imagine the strength of the tsunami that carried this boat so far inland!*

Timing a Tsunami

On May 22, 1960, an earthquake off the coast of South
America generated a tsunami
that completely crossed the
Pacific Ocean. Ten thousand
kilometers away from the
origin of the earthquake, the
tsunami hit the city of Hilo
on the coast of Hawaii, causing extensive damage.

If the tsunami traveled at
a speed of 188 m/s, how
long after the earthquake
occurred did the tsunami

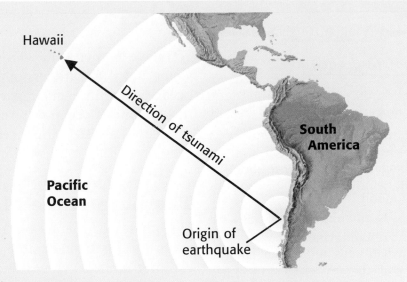

Hawaii

Direction of tsunami

Pacific
Ocean

South
America

Origin of
earthquake

reach Hilo? If the residents of
Hilo heard about the earthquake as soon as it hap-
pened, do you think they
had enough warning time?

What might be done to
ensure that this amount of
time would be sufficient
warning for a tsunami?

Storm Surges

A **storm surge** is a local rise in sea level near the shore that
is caused by strong winds from a storm, such as a hurricane.
Winds form a storm surge by blowing water into a big pile
under the storm. As the storm moves onto shore, so does the
giant mass of water beneath it. Storm surges often disappear
as quickly as they form, making them difficult to study. Storm
surges contain a lot of energy and can reach about 8 m in
height. This often makes them the most destructive part
of hurricanes.

SECTION REVIEW

1. Explain how water moves as waves travel through it.

2. Where do deep-water waves become shallow-water waves?

3. Name five events that can cause a tsunami.

4. **Doing Calculations** Look again at Figure 11. If the wave
   speed is 0.8 m/s, what is the wavelength?

internet**connect**

*SCi*_INKS_
NSTA

TOPIC: Ocean Waves
GO TO: www.scilinks.org
*sci*LINKS NUMBER: HSTE340

What You'll Do

◆ Explain tides and their relationship with the Earth, the sun, and the moon.

◆ Classify different types of tides.

◆ Analyze the relationship between tides and coastal land.

Tides

You have learned how winds and earthquakes can move ocean water. But there are less-obvious forces that continually move ocean water in regular patterns called tides. **Tides** are daily movements of ocean water that change the level of the ocean's surface. Tides are influenced by the sun and the moon, and they occur in a variety of cycles.

The Lure of the Moon

The phases of the moon and their relationship to the tides were first discovered more than 2,000 years ago by a Greek explorer named Pytheas. But Pytheas and other early investigators could not explain the relationship. A scientific explanation was not given until 1687, when Sir Isaac Newton's theories on the principle of gravitational pull were published. The gravity of the moon pulls on every particle of the Earth, but the pull is much more noticeable in liquids than in solids. This is because liquids move more easily. Even the liquid in an open soft drink is slightly pulled by the moon's gravity.

Gravitational forces from both the sun and the moon continuously pull on the Earth. Although the moon is much smaller than the sun, the moon's gravity is the dominant force behind Earth's tides.

High Tide and Low Tide How high tides get and how often they occur depend on the position of the moon as it revolves around the Earth. The moon's pull is strongest on the part of the Earth directly facing the moon. When that part happens to be a part of the ocean, the water there bulges toward the moon.

At the same time, water on the opposite side of the Earth bulges due to the motion of the Earth and the moon around each other. These bulges are called *high tides*. Notice in **Figure 18** how the position of the moon causes the water to bulge. Also notice that when high tides occur, water is drawn away from the area between the high tides, causing *low tides* to form.

Puzzled about why high tide also occurs on the side of the Earth opposite the moon? Turn to page 106 to see how you can find out for yourself.

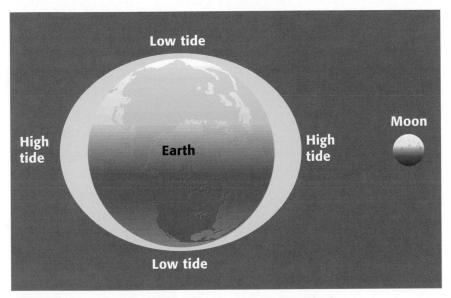

Figure 18 *High tide occurs on the part of Earth that is closest to the moon. At the same time, high tide also occurs on the opposite side of Earth.*

Timing the Tides The rotation of the Earth and the moon's revolution around the Earth determine when tides occur. If the Earth rotated at the same speed that the moon revolves around the Earth, tides would continuously occur at the same spots on Earth. But the moon revolves around the Earth much more slowly than the Earth rotates. **Figure 19** shows that it takes 24 hours and 50 minutes for a spot on Earth that is facing the moon to rotate so that it is facing the moon again.

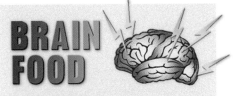

Even dry land has tides. For example, the land in Oklahoma moves up and down several centimeters throughout the day, corresponding with the tides. Tides on the solid part of Earth's surface are usually about one-third the size of ocean tides.

Tuesday, 11:00 A.M.

Wednesday, 11:50 A.M.

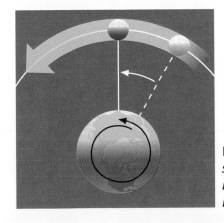

Figure 19 *Tides occur at different spots on Earth because the Earth rotates more quickly than the moon revolves around the Earth.*

Tidal Variations

The sun also affects tides. The sun is much larger than the moon, but it is also much farther away. As a result, the sun's influence on tides is less powerful than the moon's influence. The combined forces of the sun and the moon on the Earth result in tidal ranges that vary based on the positions of all three bodies. A **tidal range** is the difference between levels of ocean water at high tide and low tide.

Figure 20 *During spring tides, the gravitational forces of the sun and moon pull on the Earth either from the same direction (left) or from opposite directions (right).*

Spring Tides When the sun, Earth, and moon are in alignment with one another, spring tides occur. **Spring tides** are tides with maximum daily tidal range that occur during the new and full moons. Spring tides occur every 14 days. The first time spring tides occur is when the moon is between the sun and Earth. The second time spring tides occur is when the moon and the sun are on opposite sides of the Earth. **Figure 20** shows the positions of the sun and moon during spring tides.

Neap Tides When the sun, Earth, and moon form a 90° angle, neap tides occur. **Neap tides** are tides with minimum daily tidal range that occur during the first and third quarters of the moon. Neap tides occur halfway between the occurrence of spring tides. When neap tides occur, the gravitational forces on the Earth by the sun and the moon work against each other. **Figure 21** shows the positions of the sun and moon during neap tides.

Figure 21 *During neap tides, the sun and moon are at right angles with respect to the Earth. This arrangement minimizes their gravitational effect on the Earth.*

Tides and Topography

Tides can be accurately predicted once the tidal range has been measured at a certain point over a period of time. This information can be useful for people who live near or visit the coast, as illustrated in **Figure 22.**

Figure 22 *It's a good thing the people on the beach (left) knew when high tide occurred (right). These photos show the Bay of Fundy, in New Brunswick, Canada. The Bay of Fundy has the greatest tidal range on Earth.*

In some coastal areas with narrow inlets, movements of water called tidal bores occur. A *tidal bore* is a body of water that rushes up through a narrow bay, estuary, or river channel during the rise of high tide, causing a very sudden tidal rise. Sometimes tidal bores form waves that rush up the inlets. Tidal bores occur in coastal areas of China, the British Isles, France, and Canada.

SECTION REVIEW

1. At what two spots on Earth does high tide occur?

2. Which tides have minimum tidal range? Which tides have maximum tidal range?

3. What causes tidal bores?

4. **Applying Concepts** How many days pass between minimum and maximum tidal range in any given area? Explain.

internet**connect**

SC*i*LINKS.
NSTA

TOPIC: The Tides
GO TO: www.scilinks.org
*sci*LINKS **NUMBER:** HSTE350

Skill Builder Lab

Up from the Depths

Every year, the water in certain parts of the ocean "turns over." That is, the water at the bottom rises to the top and the water at the top falls to the bottom. This yearly change brings fresh nutrients from the bottom of the ocean to the fish living near the surface. So, it is a great time for fishing! However, the water in some parts of the ocean never turns over. You will use this activity to find out why.

Some parts of the ocean are warmer at the bottom, and some are warmer at the top. Sometimes the saltiest water is at the bottom; sometimes it is not. You will investigate how these factors help determine whether the water will turn over.

MATERIALS

- 400 mL beakers (5)
- tap water
- blue and red food coloring
- spoon
- bucket of ice
- watch or clock
- hot plate
- heat-resistant gloves
- 4 pieces of plastic wrap, approximately 30 cm × 20 cm
- salt

Ask a Question

1 Why do some parts of the ocean turn over, while others do not?

Conduct an Experiment

2 Label the beakers 1 through 5. Fill beakers 1 through 4 with tap water.

3 Add a drop of blue food coloring to the water in beakers 1 and 2 and stir.

4 Place beaker 1 in the bucket of ice for 10 minutes.

5 Add a drop of red food coloring to the water in beakers 3 and 4 and stir.

6 Set beaker 3 on a hot plate turned to a low setting for 10 minutes.

7 Add one spoonful of salt to the water in beaker 4, and stir.

8 While beaker 1 is cooling and beaker 3 is heating, copy the data table on the next page into your ScienceLog.

Observations Chart	
Mixture of water	**Observations**
Warm water placed above cold water	
Cold water placed above warm water	
Salty water placed above fresh water	DO NOT WRITE IN BOOK
Fresh water placed above salty water	

9 Pour half of the water in beaker 1 into beaker 5. Return beaker 1 to the bucket of ice.

10 Tuck a sheet of plastic wrap into beaker 5 so that the plastic rests on the surface of the water and lines the upper half of the beaker.

11 Put on your gloves. Slowly pour half of the water in beaker 3 into the plastic-lined upper half of beaker 5 to form two layers of water. Return beaker 3 to the hot plate, and remove your gloves.

12 Very carefully pull on one edge of the plastic wrap and remove it so that the warm, red water rests on the cold, blue water. **CAUTION:** The plastic wrap may be warm.

Make Observations

13 Wait about 5 minutes, and then observe the layers in beaker 5. Did one layer remain on top of the other? Was there any mixing or turning over? Record your observations in your data table.

14 Empty beaker 5 and rinse it with clean tap water.

15 Repeat the procedure in steps 9–14. This time, pour warm, red water from beaker 3 on the bottom and cold, blue water from beaker 1 on top. (Use gloves when pouring warm water.)

16 Again repeat the procedure used in steps 9–14. This time pour blue tap water from beaker 2 on the bottom and red, salty water from beaker 4 on top.

17 Repeat the procedure used in steps 9–14 a third time. This time pour red, salty water from beaker 4 on the bottom and blue tap water from beaker 2 on top.

Analyze the Results

18 Compare the results of all four trials. Explain why the water turned over in some of the trials but not in all of them.

Draw Conclusions

19 What is the effect of temperature and salinity on the density of water?

20 What makes the temperature of ocean water decrease? What could make the salinity of ocean water increase?

21 What reasons can you give to explain why some parts of the ocean turn over in the spring while some do not?

Going Further
Suggest a method for setting up a model that tests the combined effects of temperature and salinity on the density of water. Consider using more than two water samples and dyes.

Chapter Highlights

SECTION 1

Vocabulary

surface current *(p. 71)*
Coriolis effect *(p. 72)*
deep current *(p. 74)*
upwelling *(p. 77)*
El Niño *(p. 77)*

Section Notes

- Currents are classified as surface currents and deep currents.

- Surface currents are controlled by three factors: global winds, the Coriolis effect, and continental deflections.

- Surface currents, such as the Gulf Stream, can be several thousand kilometers in length.

- Deep currents form where the density of ocean water increases. Water density depends on temperature and salinity.

- Surface currents affect the climate of the land near which they flow.

SECTION 2

Vocabulary

crest *(p. 78)*
trough *(p. 78)*
wavelength *(p. 78)*
wave height *(p. 78)*
wave period *(p. 79)*
breaker *(p. 80)*
surf *(p. 80)*
whitecap *(p. 81)*
swells *(p. 81)*
tsunami *(p. 82)*
storm surge *(p. 83)*

Section Notes

- Waves are made up of two main components—crests and troughs.

- Waves are usually created by the transfer of the wind's energy across the surface of the ocean.

☑ Skills Check

Math Concepts

TWO OUT OF THREE The wave equation on page 79 has three variables. If you know two of these variables, you can figure out the third. Take a look at the examples below.

1. wave speed = 0.6 m/s, wave period = 10 s
   wavelength = wave speed × wave period
   = 6 m

2. wave speed = 0.6 m/s, wavelength = 6 m
   wave period = $\dfrac{\text{wavelength}}{\text{wave speed}}$ = 10 s

Visual Understanding

BREAKING WAVES Before shallow-water waves break, their wave height increases and their wavelength decreases. Look at Figure 12 on page 80 again. Notice that the waves are taller and that their crests are closer together near the breaker zone.

SECTION 2

- Waves travel through water near the water's surface, while the water itself rises and falls in circular movements.

- Waves travel in the direction the wind blows. If the wind blows over a long distance, the wavelength becomes very large and the waves travel quickly.

- Wind-generated waves are classified as deep-water and shallow-water waves.

- Tsunamis are dangerous waves that can be very destructive to coastal communities.

SECTION 3

Vocabulary

tides *(p. 84)*

tidal range *(p. 86)*

spring tides *(p. 86)*

neap tides *(p. 86)*

Section Notes

- Tides are caused by the gravitational forces of the moon and sun tugging on the Earth.

- The moon's gravity is the main force behind tides.

- The relative positions of the sun and moon with respect to Earth cause different tidal ranges.

- Maximum tidal range occurs during spring tides.

- Minimum tidal range occurs during neap tides.

- Tidal bores occur as high tide rises in narrow coastal inlets.

Labs

Turning the Tides *(p. 106)*

Chapter Review

For each pair of terms, explain the difference in their meaning.

1. wavelength/wave height

2. whitecap/swell

3. tsunami/storm surge

4. spring tide/neap tide

Replace the incorrect term in each of the following sentences with the correct term provided in the word bank below:

5. Deep currents are directly controlled by wind.

6. The Coriolis effect reduces upwelling along the coast of South America.

7. Neap tides occur when the moon is between the Earth and the sun.

8. A tidal bore is the difference between levels of ocean water at high tide and low tide.

Word bank: breakers, spring tides, tsunamis, surface currents, tidal range, El Niño.

UNDERSTANDING CONCEPTS

Multiple Choice

9. Surface currents are formed by
   a. the moon's gravity.
   b. the sun's gravity.
   c. wind.
   d. increased water density.

10. Deep currents form when
    a. cold air decreases water density.
    b. warm air increases water density.
    c. the ocean surface freezes and solids from the water underneath are removed.
    d. salinity increases.

11. When waves come near the shore,
    a. they speed up.
    b. they maintain their speed.
    c. their wavelength increases.
    d. their wave height increases.

12. Longshore currents transport sediment
    a. out to the open ocean.
    b. along the shore.
    c. during low tide only.
    d. during high tide only.

13. Whitecaps break
    a. in the surf.
    b. in the breaker zone.
    c. in the open ocean.
    d. as their wavelength increases.

14. Tidal range is greatest during
    a. spring tide.
    b. neap tide.
    c. a tidal bore.
    d. the day only.

Short Answer

15. Explain the relationship between upwelling and El Niño.

16. Explain what happens when the North Atlantic Deep Water meets the Antarctic Bottom Water.

17. Describe the relative positions of the Earth, the moon, and the sun during neap tide. Where do high tide and low tide occur during this time?

18. Explain the difference between the breaker zone and the surf.

Concept Mapping

19. Use the following terms to create a concept map: wind, deep currents, sun's gravity, types of ocean-water movement, surface currents, tides, increasing water density, waves, moon's gravity.

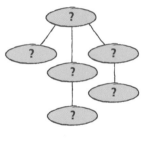

CRITICAL THINKING AND PROBLEM SOLVING

Write one or two sentences to answer the following questions:

20. What would happen to surface currents if the Earth reversed its rotation? Be specific.

21. How would you explain a bottle moving across the water in the same direction the waves are traveling?

22. You and a friend are planning a fishing trip to the ocean. Your friend tells you that the fish bite more in his secret fishing spot during low tide. If low tide occurred at the spot at 7 A.M. today and you are going to fish there in one week, at what time will low tide occur in that spot?

MATH IN SCIENCE

23. If a barrier island that is 1 km wide and 10 km long loses 1.5 m of its width per year to erosion by longshore current, how long will it take for the island to lose one-fourth of its width?

INTERPRETING GRAPHICS

Study the diagram below, and answer the questions that follow.

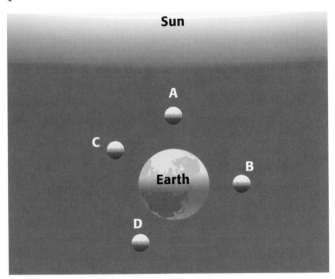

24. At which position (A, B, C, or D) would the moon be during a neap tide?

25. At which position (A, B, C, or D) would the moon be during a spring tide?

26. Would tidal range be greater with the moon at position C or position D? Why?

Reading Check-up

Take a minute to review your answers to the Pre-Reading Questions found at the bottom of page 68. Have your answers changed? If necessary, revise your answers based on what you have learned since you began this chapter.

CAREERS

SEISMOLOGIST

As a seismologist, **Hiroo Kanamori** studies how earthquakes occur and tries to reduce their impact on our society. He also analyzes the effects of earthquakes on oceans and how earthquakes cause tsunamis (tsoo NAH mes). He has discovered that even weak earthquakes can create tsunamis.

*B*ecause most tsunamis are caused by underwater earthquakes, scientists can monitor earthquakes to predict when and where a tsunami will hit land. But the predictions are not always accurate. Very weak earthquakes should not create powerful tsunamis, yet they do. Kanamori calls these special events *tsunami earthquakes,* and he has learned how to predict the size of the resulting tsunamis.

A tsunami can be more dangerous than an earthquake. When people feel the tremors created when the plates slide, they don't always realize that a large tsunami may be on the way. Because of this, people don't expect a tsunami and don't leave the area.

Measuring Tsunami Earthquakes

As tectonic plates grind against each other, they send out seismic waves. These waves travel through the earth's crust and can be recorded by a sensitive machine. But when the plates grind very slowly, only long period seismic waves are recorded. When Kanamori sees a long period wave, he knows that a tsunami will form.

"The speed of the average tsunami is about 800 km/h per hour, which is much slower than the speed of the long period waves at 15,000 km/h. So these special seismic waves arrive at distant recording stations much earlier than a tsunami," explains Kanamori. This important fact lets scientists like Kanamori warn people in the tsunami's path so they can leave the area.

An Interesting Career

Kanamori finds his work very rewarding. "It is always good to see how what we learned in the classroom can solve our real-life problems," he explains. "We can see how physics and mathematics work to explain seemingly complex natural events, such as earthquakes, volcanoes, and tsunamis."

A Challenge

▶ The depth of an ocean influences how fast a tsunami travels. To investigate, fill a 0.5 m long tub with 5 cm of water. Tap the tub. How long does it take for the wave to go back and forth? Add more water, and tap it again. Did the wave move faster or slower?

▶ *Monster waves are well-known in many communities along the Pacific coast.*

Red Tides

Imagine going to the beach only to find that the ocean water has turned red and fish are floating belly up all over the place. This is not an imaginary scene. It really happens. What could cause such widespread damage to the ocean? Single-cell algae, that's what!

Blooming Algae

When certain algae grow rapidly, they clump together on the ocean's surface in an algal bloom that changes the color of the water. People called these algal blooms red tides because the blooms often turned the water red or reddish-brown. They also believed that tidal conditions caused the blooms. Scientists now call these algae explosions harmful algal blooms (HABs) because HABs are not always red, and they are not directly related to tides. The blooms are harmful because certain species of algae produce toxins that can poison fish, shellfish, and people.

Scientists also have learned that the ocean's natural currents may carry HABs hundreds of miles along a coastline. For example, in 1987, the Gulf Stream off the Atlantic coast of Florida carried a toxic bloom up the coast to North Carolina.

Troublesome Toxins

Some people who ate tainted shellfish from the North Carolina coast in 1987 suffered from muscular aches, anxiety, sweating, dizziness, diarrhea, vomiting, and abdominal pain. Some algae toxins can even kill people who eat the tainted seafood. Another HAB occurred in 1987 in Nova Scotia, Canada. Four people died from

▲ *Harmful algal blooms are caused by algae like the one shown above right.*

eating contaminated shellfish, and another 150 people suffered from symptoms such as dizziness, headaches, seizures, short-term memory loss, and comas.

In the 1990s, Texas, Maryland, Alaska, and many other coastal states experienced HABs. However, the problem is not confined to North America. Throughout the 1990s, HABs caused health problems in South Africa, Argentina, India, New Zealand, and France.

No Signs to Read

Fish and shellfish are major sources of protein for people all over the world. Unfortunately, there are no outward signs when seafood is contaminated. The toxins don't change the flavor, and cooking the seafood doesn't eliminate the toxins. Sometimes a HAB rides into an area on an ocean current, causing fish to die and people to become ill before authorities are aware of the problem.

Fortunately, scientists all over the world are working on ways to monitor and even predict HABs. As a result, people eventually may be able to eat fish and shellfish without worrying about toxic algae.

Find Out More

▶ Some people think that human activities are causing more HABs than occurred in the past. Other people disagree. Find out more about this issue, and have a class debate about the role humans play in creating HABs.

SAFETY FIRST!

Exploring, inventing, and investigating are essential to the study of science. However, these activities can also be dangerous. To make sure that your experiments and explorations are safe, you must be aware of a variety of safety guidelines.

You have probably heard of the saying, "It is better to be safe than sorry." This is particularly true in a science classroom where experiments and explorations are being performed. Being uninformed and careless can result in serious injuries. Don't take chances with your own safety or with anyone else's.

Following are important guidelines for staying safe in the science classroom. Your teacher may also have safety guidelines and tips that are specific to your classroom and laboratory. Take the time to be safe.

Safety Rules!

Start Out Right

Always get your teacher's permission before attempting any laboratory exploration. Read the procedures carefully, and pay particular attention to safety information and caution statements. If you are unsure about what a safety symbol means, look it up or ask your teacher. You cannot be too careful when it comes to safety. If an accident does occur, inform your teacher immediately, regardless of how minor you think the accident is.

If you are instructed to note the odor of a substance, wave the fumes toward your nose with your hand. Never put your nose close to the source.

Safety Symbols

All of the experiments and investigations in this book and their related worksheets include important safety symbols to alert you to particular safety concerns. Become familiar with these symbols so that when you see them, you will know what they mean and what to do. It is important that you read this entire safety section to learn about specific dangers in the laboratory.

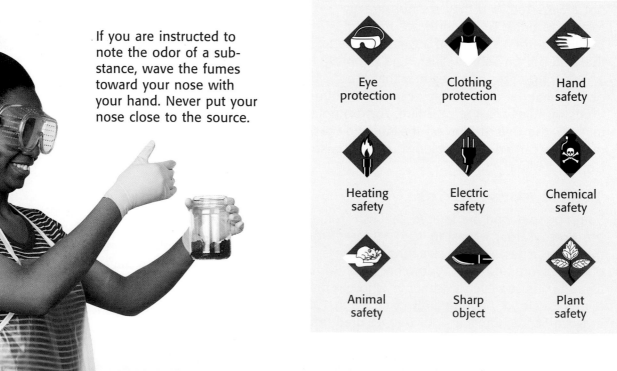

Eye protection	Clothing protection	Hand safety
Heating safety	Electric safety	Chemical safety
Animal safety	Sharp object	Plant safety

Eye Safety

Wear safety goggles when working around chemicals, acids, bases, or any type of flame or heating device. Wear safety goggles any time there is even the slightest chance that harm could come to your eyes. If any substance gets into your eyes, notify your teacher immediately, and flush your eyes with running water for at least 15 minutes. Treat any unknown chemical as if it were a dangerous chemical. Never look directly into the sun. Doing so could cause permanent blindness.

Avoid wearing contact lenses in a laboratory situation. Even if you are wearing safety goggles, chemicals can get between the contact lenses and your eyes. If your doctor requires that you wear contact lenses instead of glasses, wear eye-cup safety goggles in the lab.

Safety Equipment

Know the locations of the nearest fire alarms and any other safety equipment, such as fire blankets and eyewash fountains, as identified by your teacher, and know the procedures for using them.

Be extra careful when using any glassware. When adding a heavy object to a graduated cylinder, tilt the cylinder so the object slides slowly to the bottom.

Neatness

Keep your work area free of all unnecessary books and papers. Tie back long hair, and secure loose sleeves or other loose articles of clothing, such as ties and bows. Remove dangling jewelry. Don't wear open-toed shoes or sandals in the laboratory. Never eat, drink, or apply cosmetics in a laboratory setting. Food, drink, and cosmetics can easily become contaminated with dangerous materials.

Certain hair products (such as aerosol hair spray) are flammable and should not be worn while working near an open flame. Avoid wearing hair spray or hair gel on lab days.

Sharp/Pointed Objects

Use knives and other sharp instruments with extreme care. Never cut objects while holding them in your hands. Place objects on a suitable work surface for cutting.

Heat

Wear safety goggles when using a heating device or a flame. Whenever possible, use an electric hot plate as a heat source instead of an open flame. When heating materials in a test tube, always angle the test tube away from yourself and others. In order to avoid burns, wear heat-resistant gloves whenever instructed to do so.

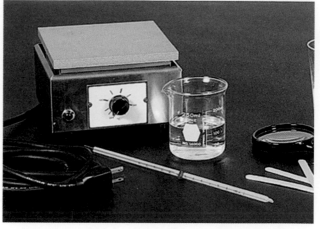

Electricity

Be careful with electrical cords. When using a microscope with a lamp, do not place the cord where it could trip someone. Do not let cords hang over a table edge in a way that could cause equipment to fall if the cord is accidentally pulled. Do not use equipment with damaged cords. Be sure your hands are dry and that the electrical equipment is in the "off" position before plugging it in. Turn off and unplug electrical equipment when you are finished.

Chemicals

Wear safety goggles when handling any potentially dangerous chemicals, acids, or bases. If a chemical is unknown, handle it as you would a dangerous chemical. Wear an apron and safety gloves when working with acids or bases or whenever you are told to do so. If a spill gets on your skin or clothing, rinse it off immediately with water for at least 5 minutes while calling to your teacher.

Never mix chemicals unless your teacher tells you to do so. Never taste, touch, or smell chemicals unless you are specifically directed to do so. Before working with a flammable liquid or gas, check for the presence of any source of flame, spark, or heat.

Animal Safety

Always obtain your teacher's permission before bringing any animal into the school building. Handle animals only as your teacher directs. Always treat animals carefully and with respect. Wash your hands thoroughly after handling any animal.

Plant Safety

Do not eat any part of a plant or plant seed used in the laboratory. Wash hands thoroughly after handling any part of a plant. When in nature, do not pick any wild plants unless your teacher instructs you to do so.

Glassware

Examine all glassware before use. Be sure that glassware is clean and free of chips and cracks. Report damaged glassware to your teacher. Glass containers used for heating should be made of heat-resistant glass.

DISCOVERY LAB

Clean Up Your Act

When you wash dishes, the family car, the bathroom sink, or your clothes, you wash them with water. But have you ever wondered how water gets clean? Two major methods of purifying water are filtration and evaporation. In this activity you will use both of these methods to test how well they remove pollutants from water. You will test detritus (decaying plant matter), soil, vinegar, and detergent. Your teacher may also ask you to test other pollutants.

Form a Hypothesis

1. Form a hypothesis about whether filtration and evaporation will clean each of the four pollutants from the water and how well they might do it. Then use the procedures below to test your hypothesis.

Part A: Filtration

Filtration is a common method of removing various pollutants from water. It requires very little energy—gravity pulls water down through the layers of filter material. See how well this energy-efficient method works to clean your sample of polluted water.

Conduct an Experiment

2. Put on your goggles. Use scissors to cut the bottom out of the empty soda bottle carefully.

3. Carefully punch four or five small holes through the plastic cap of the bottle using a small nail and hammer. Screw the plastic cap onto the bottle.

4. Turn the bottle upside down, and set its neck in a ring on a ring stand, as shown on the next page. Put a handful of gravel into the inverted bottle. Add a layer of activated charcoal, followed by thick layers of sand and gravel. Place a 400 mL beaker under the neck of the bottle.

5. Fill each of the large beakers with 1,000 mL of clean water. Set one beaker aside to serve as the control. Add three or four spoonfuls of each of the following pollutants to the other beaker: detritus, soil, household vinegar, and dishwashing detergent.

Materials

Part A

- scissors
- plastic 2 L soda bottle with cap
- hammer and small nail
- gravel
- activated charcoal
- sand

Part B

- Erlenmeyer flask
- one-hole rubber stopper with a glass tube
- 1.5 m of plastic tubing
- heat-resistant gloves
- hot plate
- sealable plastic sandwich bag
- ice

Parts A and B

- ring stand with ring
- 400 mL beaker
- 1,000 mL beakers (2)
- 2,000 mL of water
- detritus (grass and leaf clippings)
- soil
- household vinegar
- dishwashing detergent
- hand lens
- 2 plastic spoons
- pH test strips

Collect Data

6. Copy the table below into your Science-Log, and record your observations for each beaker in the columns labeled "Before cleaning."

7. Observe the color of the water in each beaker.

8. Use a hand lens to examine the water for visible particles.

9. Smell the water, and note any unusual odors.

10. Stir the water in each beaker rapidly with a plastic spoon, and check for suds. Use a different spoon for each sample.

11. Use a pH test strip to find the pH of the water.

12. Gently stir the clean water, and then pour half of it through the filtration device.

13. Observe the water in the collection beaker for color, particles, odors, suds, and pH. Be patient. It may take several minutes for the water to travel through the filtration device.

14. Record your observations in the appropriate "After filtration" column in your table.

15. Repeat steps 12–14 using the polluted water.

Results Table						
	Before cleaning (clean water)	Before cleaning (polluted water)	After filtration (clean water)	After filtration (polluted water)	After evaporation (clean water)	After evaporation (polluted water)
Color						
Particles						
Odor						
Suds						
pH						

DO NOT WRITE IN BOOK

Analyze the Results

16. How did the color of the polluted water change after the filtration? Did the color of the clean water change?

17. Did the filtration method remove all of the particles from the polluted water? Explain.

18. How much did the pH of the polluted water change? Did the pH of the clean water change? Was the final pH of the polluted water the same as the pH of the clean water before cleaning? Explain.

Part B: Evaporation

Cleaning water by evaporation is more expensive than cleaning water by filtration. Evaporation requires more energy, which can come from a variety of sources. In this activity, you will use an electric hot plate as the energy source. See how well this method works to clean your sample of polluted water.

Conduct an Experiment

19. Fill an Erlenmeyer flask with about 250 mL of the clean water, and insert the rubber stopper and glass tube into the flask.

20. Wearing goggles and gloves, connect about 1.5 m of plastic tubing to the glass tube.

21. Set the flask on the hot plate, and run the plastic tubing up and around the ring and down into a clean, empty 400 mL collection beaker.

22. Fill the sandwich bag with ice, seal the bag, and place the bag on the ring stand. Be sure the plastic bag and the tubing touch, as shown below.

23. Bring the water in the flask to a slow boil. As the water vapor passes by the bag of ice, the vapor will condense and drip into the collection beaker.

Collect Data

24. Observe the water in the collection beaker for color, particles, odor, suds, and pH. Record your observations in the appropriate "After evaporation" column in your data table.

25. Repeat steps 23–24 using the polluted water.

Analyze the Results

26. How did the color of the polluted water change after evaporation? Did the color of the clean water change after evaporation?

27. Did the evaporation method remove all of the particles from the polluted water? Explain.

28. How much did the pH of the polluted water change? Did the pH of the final clean water change? Was the final pH of the polluted water the same as the pH of the clean water before it was cleaned? Explain.

Draw Conclusions (Parts A and B)

29. Which method—filtration or evaporation—removed the most pollutants from the water? Explain your reasoning.

30. Describe any changes that occurred in the clean water during this experiment.

31. What do you think are the advantages and disadvantages of each method?

32. Explain how you think each material (sand, gravel, and charcoal) used in the filtration system helped clean the water.

33. List areas of the country where you think each method of purification would be the most and the least beneficial. Explain your reasoning.

Going Further

Do you think either purification method would remove oil from water? If time permits, repeat your experiment using several spoonfuls of cooking oil as the pollutant.

Filtration is only one step in the purification of water at water-treatment plants. Research other methods used to purify public water supplies.

Investigating an Oil Spill

Have you ever wondered why it is important to bring used motor oil to a recycling center rather than simply pouring it down the nearest drain or sewer? Or have you ever wondered why an oil spill of only a few thousand liters into an ocean containing many millions of liters of water can cause so much damage? The reason has to do with the fact that a little oil goes a long way.

Observing Oil and Water

You may have heard the expression "Oil and water don't mix." This is true—oil dropped on water will spread out thinly over the surface of the water. In this activity, you'll learn exactly how far oil can spread when it is in contact with water.

Procedure

1. Fill the pan two-thirds full with water. Be sure to wear your goggles and gloves.

2. Using the pipet, carefully add one drop of oil to the water in the middle of the pan.
   Caution: Machine oil is poisonous. Keep materials that have contacted oil out of your mouth and eyes.

3. Observe what happens to the drop of oil for the next few seconds. Record your observations in your ScienceLog.

4. Using a metric ruler, measure the diameter of the oil slick to the nearest centimeter.

5. Determine the area of the oil slick in square centimeters by using the formula for finding the area of a circle ($A = \pi r^2$). The radius (r) is equal to the diameter you measured in step 4 divided by 2. Multiply the radius by itself to get the square of the radius (r^2). Pi (π) is equal to 3.14.

   Example
   If your diameter is 10 cm,
   $r = 5$ cm, $r^2 = 25$ cm^2, $\pi = 3.14$
   $$A = \pi r^2$$
   $$A = 3.14 \times 25 \text{ cm}^2$$
   $$A = 78.5 \text{ cm}^2$$

6. Record your answers in your ScienceLog.

Materials

- safety gloves
- large pan (at least 22 cm in diameter)
- water
- pipet
- 15 mL light machine oil
- metric ruler
- graduated cylinder
- calculator (optional)

Analysis

7. What happened to the drop of oil when it came in contact with the water? Did this surprise you?

8. What total surface area was covered by the oil slick? (Be sure to show your calculations.)

9. What does this experiment tell you about the density of oil compared with the density of water? Explain.

Going Further

Can you devise a way to clean the oil from the water? Get permission from your teacher before testing your cleaning method.

Do you think oil behaves the same way in ocean water? Devise an experiment to test your hypothesis.

Finding the Number of Drops in a Liter

"It's only a few drops," you may think as you spill something toxic on the ground. But those drops eventually add up. Just how many drops does it take to make a difference? In this activity, you'll learn just what an impact a few drops can have.

Procedure

10. Using a clean pipet, count the number of water drops it takes to fill the graduated cylinder to 10 mL. Be sure to add the drops slowly so you get an accurate count.

11. Since there are 1,000 mL in a liter, multiply the number of drops in 10 mL by 100. This gives you the number of drops in a liter.

Analysis

12. How many drops of water from your pipet does it take to fill a 1 L container?

13. What would happen if someone spilled 4 L of oil into a lake?

Going Further

Find out how much oil supertankers contain. Can you imagine the size of an oil slick that would form if one of these tankers spilled its oil?

Turning the Tides

Daily tides are caused by two "bulges" on the ocean's surface— one on the side of the Earth facing the moon and the other on the opposite side. The bulge on the side facing the moon is caused by the moon's gravitational pull on the water. But the bulge on the opposite side is slightly more difficult to explain. Whereas the moon pulls the water on one side of the Earth, the combined rotation of the Earth and the moon "pushes" the water on the opposite side of the Earth. In this activity, you will model the motion of the Earth and the moon to investigate the tidal bulge on the side of Earth facing away from the moon.

Materials

- 2 disks of corrugated cardboard, one large and one small, with centers marked
- white glue
- piece of dowel, 1/4 in. in diameter and 36 cm long
- 5 cm length of string
- stapler with staples
- 1 × 1 cm piece of cardboard
- sharp pencil

Procedure

1. Draw a line from the center of each disk along the folds in the cardboard to the edge of the disk. This line is the radius.

2. Place a drop of white glue on one end of the dowel. Lay the larger disk flat, and align the dowel with the line for the radius you drew in step 1. Insert about 2.5 cm of the dowel into the edge of the disk.

3. Add a drop of glue to the other end of the dowel, and push that end into the smaller disk, again along its radius. The setup should look like a large two-headed lollipop, as shown below. This is a model of the Earth-moon system.

4. Staple the string to the edge of the large disk on the side opposite the dowel. Staple the cardboard square to the other end of the string. This smaller piece of cardboard represents the Earth's oceans that face away from the moon.

5. Place the tip of the pencil at the center of the large disk, as shown in the figure on the next page, and spin the model. You may poke a small hole in the bottom of the disk with your pencil, but DO NOT poke all the way through the cardboard. Record your observations in your ScienceLog. **Caution:** Be sure you are at a safe distance from other people before spinning your model.

6. Now find your model's *center of mass.* This is the point at which the model can be balanced on the end of the pencil. **Hint:** It might be easier to find the center of mass using the eraser end. Then use the sharpened end of the pencil to balance the model. This balance point should be just inside the edge of the larger disk.

7. Place the pencil at the center of mass, and spin the model around the pencil. Again, you may wish to poke a small hole in the disk. Record your observations in your ScienceLog.

Analysis

8. What happened when you tried to spin the model around the center of the large disk? This model, called the Earth-centered model, represents the incorrect view that the moon orbits the center of the Earth.

9. What happened when you tried to spin the model around its center of mass? This point, called the *barycenter,* is the point around which both the Earth and the moon rotate.

10. In each case, what happened to the string and cardboard square when the model was spun?

11. Which model—the Earth-centered model or the barycentric model—explains why the Earth has a tidal bulge on the side opposite the moon? Explain.

Earth

Moon

Tidal bulges

Concept Mapping: A Way to Bring Ideas Together

What Is a Concept Map?

Have you ever tried to tell someone about a book or a chapter you've just read and found that you can remember only a few isolated words and ideas? Or maybe you've memorized facts for a test and then weeks later discovered you're not even sure what topics those facts covered.

In both cases, you may have understood the ideas or concepts by themselves but not in relation to one another. If you could somehow link the ideas together, you would probably understand them better and remember them longer. This is something a concept map can help you do. A concept map is a way to see how ideas or concepts fit together. It can help you see the "big picture."

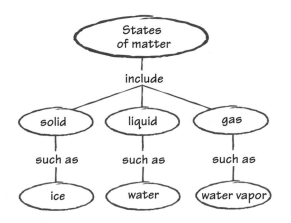

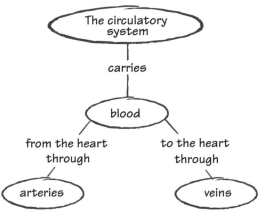

How to Make a Concept Map

1 **Make a list of the main ideas or concepts.**

It might help to write each concept on its own slip of paper. This will make it easier to rearrange the concepts as many times as necessary to make sense of how the concepts are connected. After you've made a few concept maps this way, you can go directly from writing your list to actually making the map.

2 **Arrange the concepts in order from the most general to the most specific.**

Put the most general concept at the top and circle it. Ask yourself, "How does this concept relate to the remaining concepts?" As you see the relationships, arrange the concepts in order from general to specific.

3 **Connect the related concepts with lines.**

4 **On each line, write an action word or short phrase that shows how the concepts are related.**

Look at the concept maps on this page, and then see if you can make one for the following terms:

plants, water, photosynthesis, carbon dioxide, sun's energy

One possible answer is provided at right, but don't look at it until you try the concept map yourself.

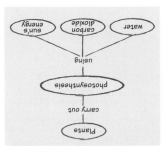

SI Measurement

The International System of Units, or SI, is the standard system of measurement used by many scientists. Using the same standards of measurement makes it easier for scientists to communicate with one another.

SI works by combining prefixes and base units. Each base unit can be used with different prefixes to define smaller and larger quantities. The table below lists common SI prefixes.

SI Prefixes			
Prefix	**Abbreviation**	**Factor**	**Example**
kilo-	k	1,000	kilogram, 1 kg = 1,000 g
hecto-	h	100	hectoliter, 1 hL = 100 L
deka-	da	10	dekameter, 1 dam = 10 m
		1	meter, liter
deci-	d	0.1	decigram, 1 dg = 0.1 g
centi-	c	0.01	centimeter, 1 cm = 0.01 m
milli-	m	0.001	milliliter, 1 mL = 0.001 L
micro-	µ	0.000 001	micrometer, 1 µm = 0.000 001 m

SI Conversion Table		
SI units	**From SI to English**	**From English to SI**
Length		
kilometer (km) = 1,000 m	1 km = 0.621 mi	1 mi = 1.609 km
meter (m) = 100 cm	1 m = 3.281 ft	1 ft = 0.305 m
centimeter (cm) = 0.01 m	1 cm = 0.394 in.	1 in. = 2.540 cm
millimeter (mm) = 0.001 m	1 mm = 0.039 in.	
micrometer (µm) = 0.000 001 m		
nanometer (nm) = 0.000 000 001 m		
Area		
square kilometer (km^2) = 100 hectares	1 km^2 = 0.386 mi^2	1 mi^2 = 2.590 km^2
hectare (ha) = 10,000 m^2	1 ha = 2.471 acres	1 acre = 0.405 ha
square meter (m^2) = 10,000 cm^2	1 m^2 = 10.765 ft^2	1 ft^2 = 0.093 m^2
square centimeter (cm^2) = 100 mm^2	1 cm^2 = 0.155 in.^{2}	1 in.^{2} = 6.452 cm^2
Volume		
liter (L) = 1,000 mL = 1 dm^3	1 L = 1.057 fl qt	1 fl qt = 0.946 L
milliliter (mL) = 0.001 L = 1 cm^3	1 mL = 0.034 fl oz	1 fl oz = 29.575 mL
microliter (µL) = 0.000 001 L		
Mass		
kilogram (kg) = 1,000 g	1 kg = 2.205 lb	1 lb = 0.454 kg
gram (g) = 1,000 mg	1 g = 0.035 oz	1 oz = 28.349 g
milligram (mg) = 0.001 g		
microgram (µg) = 0.000 001 g		

Temperature Scales

Temperature can be expressed using three different scales: Fahrenheit, Celsius, and Kelvin. The SI unit for temperature is the kelvin (K).

Although 0 K is much colder than 0°C, a change of 1 K is equal to a change of 1°C.

Three Temperature Scales

	Fahrenheit	Celsius	Kelvin
Water boils	212°	100°	373
Body temperature	98.6°	37°	310
Room temperature	68°	20°	293
Water freezes	32°	0°	273

Temperature Conversions Table

To convert	Use this equation:	Example
Celsius to Fahrenheit °C ⟶ °F	$°F = \left(\dfrac{9}{5} \times °C\right) + 32$	Convert 45°C to °F. $°F = \left(\dfrac{9}{5} \times 45°C\right) + 32 = 113°F$
Fahrenheit to Celsius °F ⟶ °C	$°C = \dfrac{5}{9} \times (°F - 32)$	Convert 68°F to °C. $°C = \dfrac{5}{9} \times (68°F - 32) = 20°C$
Celsius to Kelvin °C ⟶ K	$K = °C + 273$	Convert 45°C to K. $K = 45°C + 273 = 318\ K$
Kelvin to Celsius K ⟶ °C	$°C = K - 273$	Convert 32 K to °C. $°C = 32\ K - 273 = -241°C$

Measuring Skills

Using a Graduated Cylinder

When using a graduated cylinder to measure volume, keep the following procedures in mind:

1 Make sure the cylinder is on a flat, level surface.

2 Move your head so that your eye is level with the surface of the liquid.

3 Read the mark closest to the liquid level. On glass graduated cylinders, read the mark closest to the center of the curve in the liquid's surface.

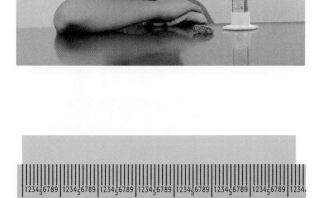

Using a Meterstick or Metric Ruler

When using a meterstick or metric ruler to measure length, keep the following procedures in mind:

1 Place the ruler firmly against the object you are measuring.

2 Align one edge of the object exactly with the zero end of the ruler.

3 Look at the other edge of the object to see which of the marks on the ruler is closest to that edge. **Note:** Each small slash between the centimeters represents a millimeter, which is one-tenth of a centimeter.

Using a Triple-Beam Balance

When using a triple-beam balance to measure mass, keep the following procedures in mind:

1 Make sure the balance is on a level surface.

2 Place all of the countermasses at zero. Adjust the balancing knob until the pointer rests at zero.

3 Place the object you wish to measure on the pan. **Caution:** Do not place hot objects or chemicals directly on the balance pan.

4 Move the largest countermass along the beam to the right until it is at the last notch that does not tip the balance. Follow the same procedure with the next-largest countermass. Then move the smallest countermass until the pointer rests at zero.

5 Add the readings from the three beams together to determine the mass of the object.

6 When determining the mass of crystals or powders, use a piece of filter paper. First find the mass of the paper. Then add the crystals or powder to the paper and re-measure. The actual mass of the crystals or powder is the total mass minus the mass of the paper. When finding the mass of liquids, first find the mass of the empty container. Then find the mass of the liquid and container together. The mass of the liquid is the total mass minus the mass of the container.

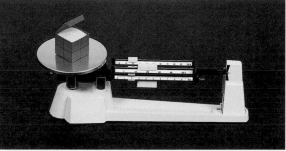

Scientific Method

The series of steps that scientists use to answer questions and solve problems is often called the **scientific method.** The scientific method is not a rigid procedure. Scientists may use all of the steps or just some of the steps of the scientific method. They may even repeat some of the steps. The goal of the scientific method is to come up with reliable answers and solutions.

Six Steps of the Scientific Method

1 **Ask a Question** Good questions come from careful **observations.** You make observations by using your senses to gather information. Sometimes you may use instruments, such as microscopes and telescopes, to extend the range of your senses. As you observe the natural world, you will discover that you have many more questions than answers. These questions drive the scientific method.

Questions beginning with *what, why, how,* and *when* are very important in focusing an investigation, and they often lead to a hypothesis. (You will learn what a hypothesis is in the next step.) Here is an example of a question that could lead to further investigation.

Question: How does acid rain affect plant growth?

2 **Form a Hypothesis** After you come up with a question, you need to turn the question into a **hypothesis.** A hypothesis is a clear statement of what you expect the answer to your question to be. Your hypothesis will represent your best "educated guess" based on your observations and what you already know. A good hypothesis is testable. If observations and information cannot be gathered or if an experiment cannot be designed to test your hypothesis, it is untestable, and the investigation can go no further.

Here is a hypothesis that could be formed from the question, "How does acid rain affect plant growth?"

Hypothesis: Acid rain causes plants to grow more slowly.

Notice that the hypothesis provides some specifics that lead to methods of testing. The hypothesis can also lead to predictions. A **prediction** is what you think will be the outcome of your experiment or data collection. Predictions are usually stated in an "if . . . then" format. For example, **if** meat is kept at room temperature, **then** it will spoil faster than meat kept in the refrigerator. More than one prediction can be made for a single hypothesis. Here is a sample prediction for the hypothesis that acid rain causes plants to grow more slowly.

Prediction: If a plant is watered with only acid rain (which has a pH of 4), then the plant will grow at half its normal rate.

3 **Test the Hypothesis** After you have formed a hypothesis and made a prediction, you should test your hypothesis. There are different ways to do this. Perhaps the most familiar way is to conduct a **controlled experiment.** A controlled experiment tests only one factor at a time. A controlled experiment has a **control group** and one or more **experimental groups.** All the factors for the control and experimental groups are the same except for one factor, which is called the **variable.** By changing only one factor, you can see the results of just that one change.

Sometimes, the nature of an investigation makes a controlled experiment impossible. For example, dinosaurs have been extinct for millions of years, and the Earth's core is surrounded by thousands of meters of rock. It would be difficult, if not impossible, to conduct controlled experiments on such things. Under such circumstances, a hypothesis may be tested by making detailed observations. Taking measurements is one way of making observations.

Test the Hypothesis

4 **Analyze the Results** After you have completed your experiments, made your observations, and collected your data, you must analyze all the information you have gathered. Tables and graphs are often used in this step to organize the data.

Analyze the Results

5 **Draw Conclusions** Based on the analysis of your data, you should conclude whether or not your results support your hypothesis. If your hypothesis is supported, you (or others) might want to repeat the observations or experiments to verify your results. If your hypothesis is not supported by the data, you may have to check your procedure for errors. You may even have to reject your hypothesis and make a new one. If you cannot draw a conclusion from your results, you may have to try the investigation again or carry out further observations or experiments.

Draw Conclusions

Do they support your hypothesis?

No

Yes

6 **Communicate Results** After any scientific investigation, you should report your results. By doing a written or oral report, you let others know what you have learned. They may want to repeat your investigation to see if they get the same results. Your report may even lead to another question, which in turn may lead to another investigation.

Communicate Results

Scientific Method in Action

The scientific method is not a "straight line" of steps. It contains loops in which several steps may be repeated over and over again, while others may not be necessary. For example, sometimes scientists will find that testing one hypothesis raises new questions and new hypotheses to be tested. And sometimes, testing the hypothesis leads directly to a conclusion. Furthermore, the steps in the scientific method are not always used in the same order. Follow the steps in the diagram below, and see how many different directions the scientific method can take you.

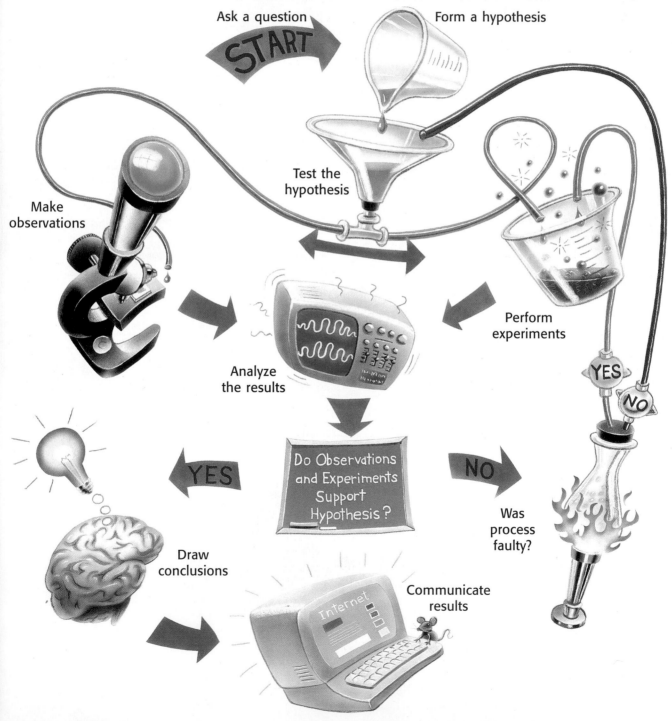

Ask a question START Form a hypothesis

Make observations

Test the hypothesis

Perform experiments

Analyze the results

YES NO

YES Do Observations and Experiments Support Hypothesis? NO

Draw conclusions

Was process faulty?

Communicate results

Internet

Making Charts and Graphs

Circle Graphs

A circle graph, or pie chart, shows how each group of data relates to all of the data. Each part of the circle represents a category of the data. The entire circle represents all of the data. For example, a biologist studying a hardwood forest in Wisconsin found that there were five different types of trees. The data table at right summarizes the biologist's findings.

Wisconsin Hardwood Trees	
Type of tree	Number found
Oak	600
Maple	750
Beech	300
Birch	1,200
Hickory	150
Total	3,000

How to Make a Circle Graph

1 In order to make a circle graph of this data, first find the percentage of each type of tree. To do this, divide the number of individual trees by the total number of trees and multiply by 100.

$$\frac{600 \text{ oak}}{3,000 \text{ trees}} \times 100 = 20\%$$

$$\frac{750 \text{ maple}}{3,000 \text{ trees}} \times 100 = 25\%$$

$$\frac{300 \text{ beech}}{3,000 \text{ trees}} \times 100 = 10\%$$

$$\frac{1,200 \text{ birch}}{3,000 \text{ trees}} \times 100 = 40\%$$

$$\frac{150 \text{ hickory}}{3,000 \text{ trees}} \times 100 = 5\%$$

2 Now determine the size of the pie shapes that make up the chart. Do this by multiplying each percentage by 360°. Remember that a circle contains 360°.

$20\% \times 360° = 72°$ $25\% \times 360° = 90°$
$10\% \times 360° = 36°$ $40\% \times 360° = 144°$
$5\% \times 360° = 18°$

3 Then check that the sum of the percentages is 100 and the sum of the degrees is 360.

$20\% + 25\% + 10\% + 40\% + 5\% = 100\%$
$72° + 90° + 36° + 144° + 18° = 360°$

4 Use a compass to draw a circle and mark its center.

5 Then use a protractor to draw angles of 72°, 90°, 36°, 144°, and 18° in the circle.

6 Finally, label each part of the graph, and choose an appropriate title.

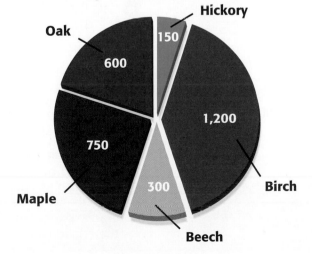

A Community of Wisconsin Hardwood Trees

Population of Appleton, 1900–2000	
Year	Population
1900	1,800
1920	2,500
1940	3,200
1960	3,900
1980	4,600
2000	5,300

Line Graphs

Line graphs are most often used to demonstrate continuous change. For example, Mr. Smith's science class analyzed the population records for their hometown, Appleton, between 1900 and 2000. Examine the data at left.

Because the year and the population change, they are the *variables*. The population is determined by, or dependent on, the year. Therefore, the population is called the **dependent variable**, and the year is called the **independent variable**. Each set of data is called a **data pair**. To prepare a line graph, data pairs must first be organized in a table like the one at left.

How to Make a Line Graph

1 Place the independent variable along the horizontal (*x*) axis. Place the dependent variable along the vertical (*y*) axis.

2 Label the *x*-axis "Year" and the *y*-axis "Population." Look at your largest and smallest values for the population. Determine a scale for the *y*-axis that will provide enough space to show these values. You must use the same scale for the entire length of the axis. Find an appropriate scale for the *x*-axis too.

3 Choose reasonable starting points for each axis.

4 Plot the data pairs as accurately as possible.

5 Choose a title that accurately represents the data.

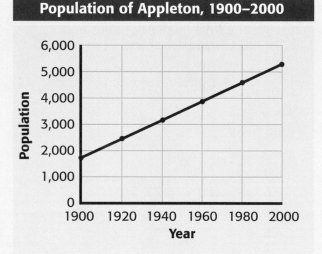

How to Determine Slope

Slope is the ratio of the change in the *y*-axis to the change in the *x*-axis, or "rise over run."

1 Choose two points on the line graph. For example, the population of Appleton in 2000 was 5,300 people. Therefore, you can define point *a* as (2000, 5,300). In 1900, the population was 1,800 people. Define point *b* as (1900, 1,800).

2 Find the change in the *y*-axis.
(*y* at point *a*) − (*y* at point *b*)
5,300 people − 1,800 people = 3,500 people

3 Find the change in the *x*-axis.
(*x* at point *a*) − (*x* at point *b*)
2000 − 1900 = 100 years

4 Calculate the slope of the graph by dividing the change in *y* by the change in *x*.

$$\text{slope} = \frac{\text{change in } y}{\text{change in } x}$$

$$\text{slope} = \frac{3{,}500 \text{ people}}{100 \text{ years}}$$

slope = 35 people per year

In this example, the population in Appleton increased by a fixed amount each year. The graph of this data is a straight line. Therefore, the relationship is **linear**. When the graph of a set of data is not a straight line, the relationship is **nonlinear**.

Using Algebra to Determine Slope

The equation in step 4 may also be arranged to be:

$$y = kx$$

where y represents the change in the y-axis, k represents the slope, and x represents the change in the x-axis.

$$\text{slope} = \frac{\text{change in } y}{\text{change in } x}$$

$$k = \frac{y}{x}$$

$$k \times x = \frac{y \times x}{x}$$

$$kx = y$$

Bar Graphs

Bar graphs are used to demonstrate change that is not continuous. These graphs can be used to indicate trends when the data are taken over a long period of time. A meteorologist gathered the precipitation records at right for Hartford, Connecticut, for April 1–15, 1996, and used a bar graph to represent the data.

Precipitation in Hartford, Connecticut April 1–15, 1996

Date	Precipitation (cm)	Date	Precipitation (cm)
April 1	0.5	April 9	0.25
April 2	1.25	April 10	0.0
April 3	0.0	April 11	1.0
April 4	0.0	April 12	0.0
April 5	0.0	April 13	0.25
April 6	0.0	April 14	0.0
April 7	0.0	April 15	6.50
April 8	1.75		

How to Make a Bar Graph

❶ Use an appropriate scale and a reasonable starting point for each axis.

❷ Label the axes, and plot the data.

❸ Choose a title that accurately represents the data.

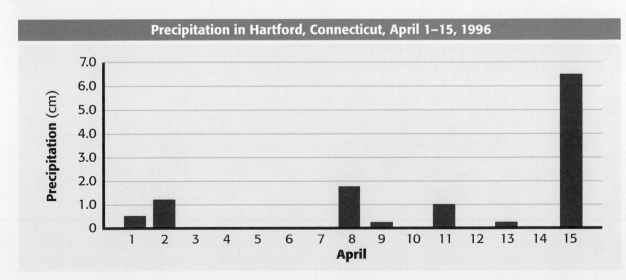

Precipitation in Hartford, Connecticut, April 1–15, 1996

Math Refresher

Science requires an understanding of many math concepts. The following pages will help you review some important math skills.

Averages

An **average**, or **mean**, simplifies a list of numbers into a single number that *approximates* their value.

> **Example:** Find the average of the following set of numbers: 5, 4, 7, and 8.

Step 1: Find the sum.

$$5 + 4 + 7 + 8 = 24$$

Step 2: Divide the sum by the amount of numbers in your set. Because there are four numbers in this example, divide the sum by 4.

$$\frac{24}{4} = 6$$

The average, or mean, is **6.**

Ratios

A **ratio** is a comparison between numbers, and it is usually written as a fraction.

> **Example:** Find the ratio of thermometers to students if you have 36 thermometers and 48 students in your class.

Step 1: Make the ratio.

$$\frac{36 \text{ thermometers}}{48 \text{ students}}$$

Step 2: Reduce the fraction to its simplest form.

$$\frac{36}{48} = \frac{36 \div 12}{48 \div 12} = \frac{3}{4}$$

The ratio of thermometers to students is **3 to 4,** or $\frac{3}{4}$. The ratio may also be written in the form 3:4.

Proportions

A **proportion** is an equation that states that two ratios are equal.

$$\frac{3}{1} = \frac{12}{4}$$

To solve a proportion, first multiply across the equal sign. This is called cross-multiplication. If you know three of the quantities in a proportion, you can use cross-multiplication to find the fourth.

> **Example:** Imagine that you are making a scale model of the solar system for your science project. The diameter of Jupiter is 11.2 times the diameter of the Earth. If you are using a plastic-foam ball with a diameter of 2 cm to represent the Earth, what diameter does the ball representing Jupiter need to be?
>
> $$\frac{11.2}{1} = \frac{x}{2 \text{ cm}}$$

Step 1: Cross-multiply.

$$\frac{11.2}{1} \diagdown\!\!\!\!\diagup \frac{x}{2}$$

$$11.2 \times 2 = x \times 1$$

Step 2: Multiply.

$$22.4 = x \times 1$$

Step 3: Isolate the variable by dividing both sides by 1.

$$x = \frac{22.4}{1}$$

$$x = 22.4 \text{ cm}$$

You will need to use a ball with a diameter of **22.4 cm** to represent Jupiter.

Percentages

A **percentage** is a ratio of a given number to 100.

Example: What is 85 percent of 40?

Step 1: Rewrite the percentage by moving the decimal point two places to the left.

$$.85$$

Step 2: Multiply the decimal by the number you are calculating the percentage of.

$$0.85 \times 40 = 34$$

85 percent of 40 is **34.**

Decimals

To **add** or **subtract decimals,** line up the digits vertically so that the decimal points line up. Then add or subtract the columns from right to left, carrying or borrowing numbers as necessary.

Example: Add the following numbers: 3.1415 and 2.96.

Step 1: Line up the digits vertically so that the decimal points line up.

$$\begin{array}{r} 3.1415 \\ + 2.96 \\ \hline \end{array}$$

Step 2: Add the columns from right to left, carrying when necessary.

$$\begin{array}{r} 1\ 1 \\ 3.1415 \\ + 2.96 \\ \hline 6.1015 \end{array}$$

The sum is **6.1015.**

Fractions

Numbers tell you how many; **fractions** tell you *how much of a whole.*

Example: Your class has 24 plants. Your teacher instructs you to put 5 in a shady spot. What fraction does this represent?

Step 1: Write a fraction with the total number of parts in the whole as the denominator.

$$\frac{?}{24}$$

Step 2: Write the number of parts of the whole being represented as the numerator.

$$\frac{5}{24}$$

$\frac{5}{24}$ of the plants will be in the shade.

Reducing Fractions

It is usually best to express a fraction in simplest form. This is called *reducing* a fraction.

Example: Reduce the fraction $\frac{30}{45}$ to its simplest form.

Step 1: Find the largest whole number that will divide evenly into both the numerator and denominator. This number is called the greatest common factor (GCF).

factors of the numerator 30: 1, 2, 3, 5, 6, 10, **15,** 30

factors of the denominator 45: 1, 3, 5, 9, **15,** 45

Step 2: Divide both the numerator and the denominator by the GCF, which in this case is 15.

$$\frac{30}{45} = \frac{30 \div 15}{45 \div 15} = \frac{2}{3}$$

$\frac{30}{45}$ reduced to its simplest form is $\frac{2}{3}$.

APPENDIX

Adding and Subtracting Fractions

To **add** or **subtract fractions** that have the **same denominator,** simply add or subtract the numerators.

Examples:

$$\frac{3}{5} + \frac{1}{5} = ? \text{ and } \frac{3}{4} - \frac{1}{4} = ?$$

Step 1: Add or subtract the numerators.

$$\frac{3}{5} + \frac{1}{5} = \frac{4}{} \text{ and } \frac{3}{4} - \frac{1}{4} = \frac{2}{}$$

Step 2: Write the sum or difference over the denominator.

$$\frac{3}{5} + \frac{1}{5} = \frac{4}{5} \text{ and } \frac{3}{4} - \frac{1}{4} = \frac{2}{4}$$

Step 3: If necessary, reduce the fraction to its simplest form.

$$\frac{4}{5} \text{ cannot be reduced, and } \frac{2}{4} = \frac{1}{2}.$$

To **add** or **subtract fractions** that have **different denominators,** first find the least common denominator (LCD).

Examples:

$$\frac{1}{2} + \frac{1}{6} = ? \text{ and } \frac{3}{4} - \frac{2}{3} = ?$$

Step 1: Write the equivalent fractions with a common denominator.

$$\frac{3}{6} + \frac{1}{6} = ? \text{ and } \frac{9}{12} - \frac{8}{12} = ?$$

Step 2: Add or subtract.

$$\frac{3}{6} + \frac{1}{6} = \frac{4}{6} \text{ and } \frac{9}{12} - \frac{8}{12} = \frac{1}{12}$$

Step 3: If necessary, reduce the fraction to its simplest form.

$$\frac{4}{6} = \frac{2}{3}, \text{ and } \frac{1}{12} \text{ cannot be reduced.}$$

Multiplying Fractions

To **multiply fractions,** multiply the numerators and the denominators together, and then reduce the fraction to its simplest form.

Example:

$$\frac{5}{9} \times \frac{7}{10} = ?$$

Step 1: Multiply the numerators and denominators.

$$\frac{5}{9} \times \frac{7}{10} = \frac{5 \times 7}{9 \times 10} = \frac{35}{90}$$

Step 2: Reduce.

$$\frac{35}{90} = \frac{35 \div 5}{90 \div 5} = \frac{7}{18}$$

Dividing Fractions

To **divide fractions**, first rewrite the divisor (the number you divide *by*) upside down. This is called the reciprocal of the divisor. Then you can multiply and reduce if necessary.

Example:

$$\frac{5}{8} \div \frac{3}{2} = ?$$

Step 1: Rewrite the divisor as its reciprocal.

$$\frac{3}{2} \rightarrow \frac{2}{3}$$

Step 2: Multiply.

$$\frac{5}{8} \times \frac{2}{3} = \frac{5 \times 2}{8 \times 3} = \frac{10}{24}$$

Step 3: Reduce.

$$\frac{10}{24} = \frac{10 \div 2}{24 \div 2} = \frac{5}{12}$$

Scientific Notation

Scientific notation is a short way of representing very large and very small numbers without writing all of the place-holding zeros.

Example: Write 653,000,000 in scientific notation.

Step 1: Write the number without the place-holding zeros.

653

Step 2: Place the decimal point after the first digit.

6.53

Step 3: Find the exponent by counting the number of places that you moved the decimal point.

6.53000000

The decimal point was moved eight places to the left. Therefore, the exponent of 10 is positive 8. Remember, if the decimal point had moved to the right, the exponent would be negative.

Step 4: Write the number in scientific notation.

$$\mathbf{6.53 \times 10^8}$$

Area

Area is the number of square units needed to cover the surface of an object.

Formulas:
Area of a square = side $\times$ side
Area of a rectangle = length $\times$ width
Area of a triangle = $\frac{1}{2} \times$ base $\times$ height

Examples: Find the areas.

Triangle
Area = $\frac{1}{2} \times$ base $\times$ height
Area = $\frac{1}{2} \times$ 3 cm $\times$ 4 cm
Area = **6 cm²**

4 cm

3 cm

Rectangle
Area = length $\times$ width
Area = 6 cm $\times$ 3 cm
Area = **18 cm²**

3 cm

6 cm

Square
Area = side $\times$ side
Area = 3 cm $\times$ 3 cm
Area = **9 cm²**

3 cm

3 cm

Volume

Volume is the amount of space something occupies.

Formulas:
Volume of a cube = side $\times$ side $\times$ side

Volume of a prism = area of base $\times$ height

Examples:
Find the volume of the solids.

Cube
Volume = side $\times$ side $\times$ side
Volume = 4 cm $\times$ 4 cm $\times$ 4 cm
Volume = **64 cm³**

4 cm

4 cm

4 cm

4 cm

3 cm

5 cm

Prism
Volume = area of base $\times$ height
Volume = (area of triangle) $\times$ height
Volume = $\left(\frac{1}{2} \times 3 \text{ cm} \times 4 \text{ cm} \right) \times 5$ cm
Volume = 6 cm² $\times$ 5 cm
Volume = **30 cm³**

Periodic Table of the Elements

Each square on the table includes an element's name, chemical symbol, atomic number, and atomic mass.

Atomic number ———— 6

Chemical symbol ———— C

Element name ———— Carbon

Atomic mass ———— 12.0

The background color indicates the type of element. Carbon is a nonmetal.

The color of the chemical symbol indicates the physical state at room temperature. Carbon is a solid.

Background

Metals	
Metalloids	
Nonmetals	

Chemical Symbol

Solid	
Liquid	
Gas	

Period 1

| 1 |
| H |
| Hydrogen |
| 1.0 |

	Group 1	Group 2
Period 2	3 Li Lithium 6.9	4 Be Beryllium 9.0
Period 3	11 Na Sodium 23.0	12 Mg Magnesium 24.3

	Group 1	Group 2	Group 3	Group 4	Group 5	Group 6	Group 7	Group 8	Group 9
Period 4	19 K Potassium 39.1	20 Ca Calcium 40.1	21 Sc Scandium 45.0	22 Ti Titanium 47.9	23 V Vanadium 50.9	24 Cr Chromium 52.0	25 Mn Manganese 54.9	26 Fe Iron 55.8	27 Co Cobalt 58.9
Period 5	37 Rb Rubidium 85.5	38 Sr Strontium 87.6	39 Y Yttrium 88.9	40 Zr Zirconium 91.2	41 Nb Niobium 92.9	42 Mo Molybdenum 95.9	43 Tc Technetium (97.9)	44 Ru Ruthenium 101.1	45 Rh Rhodium 102.9
Period 6	55 Cs Cesium 132.9	56 Ba Barium 137.3	57 La Lanthanum 138.9	72 Hf Hafnium 178.5	73 Ta Tantalum 180.9	74 W Tungsten 183.8	75 Re Rhenium 186.2	76 Os Osmium 190.2	77 Ir Iridium 192.2
Period 7	87 Fr Francium (223.0)	88 Ra Radium (226.0)	89 Ac Actinium (227.0)	104 Rf Rutherfordium (261.1)	105 Db Dubnium (262.1)	106 Sg Seaborgium (263.1)	107 Bh Bohrium (262.1)	108 Hs Hassium (265)	109 Mt Meitnerium (266)

A row of elements is called a period.

A column of elements is called a group or family.

Lanthanides

| 58 Ce Cerium 140.1 | 59 Pr Praseodymium 140.9 | 60 Nd Neodymium 144.2 | 61 Pm Promethium (144.9) | 62 Sm Samarium 150.4 |

Actinides

| 90 Th Thorium 232.0 | 91 Pa Protactinium 231.0 | 92 U Uranium 238.0 | 93 Np Neptunium (237.0) | 94 Pu Plutonium 244.1 |

These elements are placed below the table to allow the table to be narrower.

This zigzag line reminds you where the metals, nonmetals, and metalloids are.

Group 18

| | | | | | | | **Group 18** |

Periodic table elements:

Group 10	Group 11	Group 12	Group 13	Group 14	Group 15	Group 16	Group 17	Group 18
								2 **He** Helium 4.0
			5 **B** Boron 10.8	6 **C** Carbon 12.0	7 **N** Nitrogen 14.0	8 **O** Oxygen 16.0	9 **F** Fluorine 19.0	10 **Ne** Neon 20.2
			13 **Al** Aluminum 27.0	14 **Si** Silicon 28.1	15 **P** Phosphorus 31.0	16 **S** Sulfur 32.1	17 **Cl** Chlorine 35.5	18 **Ar** Argon 39.9
28 **Ni** Nickel 58.7	29 **Cu** Copper 63.5	30 **Zn** Zinc 65.4	31 **Ga** Gallium 69.7	32 **Ge** Germanium 72.6	33 **As** Arsenic 74.9	34 **Se** Selenium 79.0	35 **Br** Bromine 79.9	36 **Kr** Krypton 83.8
46 **Pd** Palladium 106.4	47 **Ag** Silver 107.9	48 **Cd** Cadmium 112.4	49 **In** Indium 114.8	50 **Sn** Tin 118.7	51 **Sb** Antimony 121.8	52 **Te** Tellurium 127.6	53 **I** Iodine 126.9	54 **Xe** Xenon 131.3
78 **Pt** Platinum 195.1	79 **Au** Gold 197.0	80 **Hg** Mercury 200.6	81 **Tl** Thallium 204.4	82 **Pb** Lead 207.2	83 **Bi** Bismuth 209.0	84 **Po** Polonium (209.0)	85 **At** Astatine (210.0)	86 **Rn** Radon (222.0)
110 **Uun*** Ununnilium (271)	111 **Uuu*** Unununium (272)	112 **Uub*** Ununbium (277)		114 **Uuq*** Ununquadium (285)		116 **Uuh*** Ununhexium (289)		118 **Uuo*** Ununoctium (293)

A number in parenthesis is the mass number of the most stable form of that element.

63 **Eu** Europium 152.0	64 **Gd** Gadolinium 157.3	65 **Tb** Terbium 158.9	66 **Dy** Dysprosium 162.5	67 **Ho** Holmium 164.9	68 **Er** Erbium 167.3	69 **Tm** Thulium 168.9	70 **Yb** Ytterbium 173.0	71 **Lu** Lutetium 175.0
95 **Am** Americium (243.1)	96 **Cm** Curium (247.1)	97 **Bk** Berkelium (247.1)	98 **Cf** Californium (251.1)	99 **Es** Einsteinium (252.1)	100 **Fm** Fermium (257.1)	101 **Md** Mendelevium (258.1)	102 **No** Nobelium (259.1)	103 **Lr** Lawrencium (262.1)

The official names and symbols for the elements greater than 109 will eventually be approved by a committee of scientists.

Physical Laws and Equations

Law of Conservation of Energy

The law of conservation of energy states that energy can be neither created nor destroyed.

The total amount of energy in a closed system is always the same. Energy can be changed from one form to another, but all the different forms of energy in a system always add up to the same total amount of energy, no matter how many energy conversions occur.

Law of Universal Gravitation

The law of universal gravitation states that all objects in the universe attract each other by a force called gravity. The size of the force depends on the masses of the objects and the distance between them.

The first part of the law explains why a bowling ball is much harder to lift than a table-tennis ball. Because the bowling ball has a much larger mass than the table-tennis ball, the amount of gravity between the Earth and the bowling ball is greater than the amount of gravity between the Earth and the table-tennis ball.

The second part of the law explains why a satellite can remain in orbit around the Earth. The satellite is carefully placed at a distance great enough to prevent the Earth's gravity from immediately pulling it down but small enough to prevent it from completely escaping the Earth's gravity and wandering off into space.

Newton's Laws of Motion

Newton's first law of motion states that an object at rest remains at rest and an object in motion remains in motion at constant speed and in a straight line unless acted on by an unbalanced force.

The first part of the law explains why a football will remain on a tee until it is kicked off or until a gust of wind blows it off.

The second part of the law explains why a bike's rider will continue moving forward after the bike tire runs into a crack in the sidewalk and the bike comes to an abrupt stop until gravity and the sidewalk stop the rider.

Newton's second law of motion states that the acceleration of an object depends on the mass of the object and the amount of force applied.

The first part of the law explains why the acceleration of a 4 kg bowling ball will be greater than the acceleration of a 6 kg bowling ball if the same force is applied to both.

The second part of the law explains why the acceleration of a bowling ball will be larger if a larger force is applied to it.

The relationship of acceleration (a) to mass (m) and force (F) can be expressed mathematically by the following equation:

$$\text{acceleration} = \frac{force}{mass} \quad \text{or} \quad a = \frac{F}{m}$$

This equation is often rearranged to the form:

$$\text{force} = \text{mass} \times \text{acceleration}$$
$$\text{or}$$
$$F = m \times a$$

Newton's third law of motion states that whenever one object exerts a force on a second object, the second object exerts an equal and opposite force on the first.

This law explains that a runner is able to move forward because of the equal and opposite force the ground exerts on the runner's foot after each step.

Useful Equations

Average speed

$$\text{Average speed} = \frac{\text{total distance}}{\text{total time}}$$

Example: A bicycle messenger traveled a distance of 136 km in 8 hours. What was the messenger's average speed?

$$\frac{136 \text{ km}}{8 \text{ h}} = 17 \text{ km/h}$$

The messenger's average speed was **17 km/h.**

Average acceleration

$$\frac{\text{Average}}{\text{acceleration}} = \frac{\text{final velocity} - \text{starting velocity}}{\text{time it takes to change velocity}}$$

Example: Calculate the average acceleration of an Olympic 100 m dash sprinter who reaches a velocity of 15 m/s south at the finish line. The race was in a straight line and lasted 10 s.

$$\frac{15 \text{ m/s} - 0 \text{ m/s}}{10 \text{ s}} = 1.5 \text{ m/s/s}$$

The sprinter's average acceleration is **1.5 m/s/s south.**

Net force

Forces in the Same Direction
When forces are in the same direction, add the forces together to determine the net force.

Example: Calculate the net force on a stalled car that is being pushed by two people. One person is pushing with a force of 13 N north-west and the other person is pushing with a force of 8 N in the same direction.

$$13 \text{ N} + 8 \text{ N} = 21 \text{ N}$$

The net force is **21 N northwest.**

Forces in Opposite Directions
When forces are in opposite directions, subtract the smaller force from the larger force to determine the net force.

Net force (cont'd)

Example: Calculate the net force on a rope that is being pulled on each end. One person is pulling on one end of the rope with a force of 12 N south. Another person is pulling on the opposite end of the rope with a force of 7 N north.

$$12 \text{ N} - 7 \text{ N} = 5 \text{ N}$$

The net force is **5 N south.**

Density

$$\text{Density} = \frac{\text{mass}}{\text{volume}}$$

Example: Calculate the density of a sponge with a mass of 10 g and a volume of 40 mL.

$$\frac{10 \text{ g}}{40 \text{ mL}} = 0.25 \text{ g/mL}$$

The density of the sponge is **0.25 g/mL.**

Pressure

Pressure is the force exerted over a given area. The SI unit for pressure is the pascal, which is abbreviated Pa.

$$\text{Pressure} = \frac{\text{force}}{\text{area}}$$

Example: Calculate the pressure of the air in a soccer ball if the air exerts a force of 10 N over an area of 0.5 m^2.

$$\text{Pressure} = \frac{10 \text{ N}}{0.5 \text{ m}^2} = 20 \text{ N/m}^2 = 20 \text{ Pa}$$

The pressure of the air inside of the soccer ball is **20 Pa.**

Concentration

$$\text{Concentration} = \frac{\text{mass of solute}}{\text{volume of solvent}}$$

Example: Calculate the concentration of a solution in which 10 g of sugar is dissolved in 125 mL of water.

$$\frac{10 \text{ g of sugar}}{125 \text{ mL of water}} = 0.08 \text{ g/mL}$$

The concentration of this solution is **0.08 g/mL.**

Properties of Common Minerals

Mineral	Color	Luster	Streak	Hardness
Silicate Minerals				
Beryl	deep green, pink, white, bluish green, or light yellow	vitreous	none	7.5–8
Chlorite	green	vitreous to pearly	pale green	2–2.5
Garnet	green or red	vitreous	none	6.5–7.5
Hornblende	dark green, brown, or black	vitreous or silky	none	5–6
Muscovite	colorless, gray, or brown	vitreous or pearly	white	2–2.5
Olivine	olive green	vitreous	none	6.5–7
Orthoclase	colorless, white, pink, or other colors	vitreous to pearly	white or none	6
Plagioclase	blue gray to white	vitreous	white	6
Quartz	colorless or white; any color when not pure	vitreous or waxy	white or none	7
Native Elements				
Copper	copper-red	metallic	copper-red	2.5–3
Diamond	pale yellow or colorless	vitreous	none	10
Graphite	black to gray	submetallic	black	1–2
Carbonates				
Aragonite	colorless, white, or pale yellow	vitreous	white	3.5–4
Calcite	colorless or white to tan	vitreous	white	3
Halides				
Fluorite	light green, yellow, purple, bluish green, or other colors	vitreous	none	4
Halite	colorless or gray	vitreous	white	2.5–3
Oxides				
Hematite	reddish brown to black	metallic to earthy	red to red-brown	5.6–6.5
Magnetite	iron black	metallic	black	5–6
Sulfates				
Anhydrite	colorless, bluish, or violet	vitreous to pearly	white	3–3.5
Gypsum	white, pink, gray, or colorless	vitreous, pearly, or silky	white	1–2.5
Sulfides				
Galena	lead gray	metallic	lead gray to black	2.5
Pyrite	brassy yellow	metallic	greenish, brownish, or black	6–6.5

Silicate Minerals / Nonsilicate Minerals

Density (g/cm³)	Cleavage, Fracture, Special Properties	Common Uses
2.6–2.8	1 cleavage direction; irregular fracture; some varieties fluoresce in ultraviolet light	gemstones, ore of the metal beryllium
2.6–3.3	1 cleavage direction; irregular fracture	
4.2	no cleavage; conchoidal to splintery fracture	gemstones, abrasives
3.2	2 cleavage directions; hackly to splintery fracture	
2.7–3	1 cleavage direction; irregular fracture	electrical insulation, wallpaper, fireproofing material, lubricant
3.2–3.3	no cleavage; conchoidal fracture	gemstones, casting
2.6	2 cleavage directions; irregular fracture	porcelain
2.6–2.7	2 cleavage directions; irregular fracture	ceramics
2.6	no cleavage; conchoidal fracture	gemstones, concrete, glass, porcelain, sandpaper, lenses
8.9	no cleavage; hackly fracture	wiring, brass, bronze, coins
3.5	4 cleavage directions; irregular to conchoidal fracture	gemstones, drilling
2.3	1 cleavage direction; irregular fracture	pencils, paints, lubricants, batteries
2.95	2 cleavage directions; irregular fracture; reacts with hydrochloric acid	minor source of barium
2.7	3 cleavage directions; irregular fracture; reacts with weak acid, double refraction	cements, soil conditioner, whitewash, construction materials
3.2	4 cleavage directions; irregular fracture; some varieties fluoresce or double refract	hydrochloric acid, steel, glass, fiberglass, pottery, enamel
2.2	3 cleavage directions; splintery to conchoidal fracture; salty taste	tanning hides, fertilizer, salting icy roads, food preservation
5.25	no cleavage; splintery fracture; magnetic when heated	iron ore for steel, gemstones, pigments
5.2	2 cleavage directions; splintery fracture; magnetic	iron ore
2.89–2.98	3 cleavage directions; conchoidal to splintery fracture	soil conditioner, sulfuric acid
2.2–2.4	3 cleavage directions; conchoidal to splintery fracture	plaster of Paris, wallboard, soil conditioner
7.4–7.6	3 cleavage directions; irregular fracture	batteries, paints
5	no cleavage; conchoidal to splintery fracture	dyes, inks, gemstones

Glossary

A

abyssal (uh BIS uhl) **plain** the broad, flat portion of the deep-ocean basin (42)

alluvial (uh LOO vee uhl) **fan** fan-shaped deposits of alluvium that form on dry land (13)

alluvium (uh LOO vee uhm) rock and soil deposited by streams (11)

aquifer (AHK wuh fuhr) a rock layer that stores and allows the flow of ground water (14)

artesian (ahr TEE zhuhn) **spring** a spring that forms where cracks occur naturally in the cap rock and the pressurized water in the aquifer flows through the cracks to the surface (16)

B

benthic environment the ocean floor and all the organisms that live on or in it; also known as the bottom environment (47)

benthos organisms that live on or in the ocean floor (46)

breaker a heightened water wave that begins to tumble downward, or break, upon nearing the shore (80)

C

channel the path a stream follows (7)

cleavage (KLEEV ij) the tendency of a mineral to break along flat surfaces (127)

condensation the change of state from a gas to a liquid (39)

continental margin the portion of the Earth's surface beneath the ocean that is made of continental crust (42)

continental rise the base of the continental slope (42)

continental shelf the flattest part of the continental margin (42)

continental slope the steepest part of the continental margin (42)

Coriolis (KOHR ee OH lis) **effect** the curving of moving objects from a straight path due to the Earth's rotation (72)

crest the highest point of a wave (78)

D

deep current a streamlike movement of ocean water far below the surface (74)

deep-ocean basin the portion of the Earth's surface beneath the ocean that is made of oceanic crust (42)

delta a fan-shaped deposit of alluvium at the mouth of a stream, where the stream empties into a large body of water (12)

density the amount of matter in a given space; mass per unit volume (125)

deposition the process by which material is dropped or settles (11)

desalination the process of evaporating sea water so that the water and the salt separate (53)

discharge the amount of water a stream or river carries in a given amount of time (7)

divide an area of higher ground that separates drainage basins (6)

drainage basin the land drained by a river system, which includes the main river and all of its tributaries (6)

E

El Niño periodic change in the location of warm and cool surface waters in the Pacific Ocean (77)

erosion the removal and transport of material by wind, water, or ice (4)

evaporation the change of state from a liquid to a vapor (39)

F

flood plain an area along a river formed from sediments deposited by floods (13)

G

gradient a measure of the change in elevation over a certain distance (7)

ground water water that is located within rocks below the Earth's surface (14)

H

hypothesis a possible explanation or answer to a question (112)

I

iceberg a large piece of ice that breaks off an ice shelf and drifts into the ocean (67)

L

load the materials carried in a stream's water (8)

longshore current the movement of water near and parallel to the shoreline (81)

M

mid-ocean ridge a long mountain chain that forms on the ocean floor where tectonic plates pull apart; usually extends along the center of ocean basins (43)

N

neap tides tides with minimum daily tidal range that occur during the first and third quarters of the moon (86)

nekton (NEK TAHN) free-swimming organisms of the ocean (46)

nonpoint-source pollution pollution that comes from many sources and that cannot be traced to specific sites (19, 56)

nonrenewable resource a natural resource that cannot be replaced or that can be replaced only over thousands or millions of years (22, 52)

nonsilicate mineral a mineral that does not contain compounds of silicon and oxygen (126)

O

ocean trench a seemingly bottomless crack in the deep-ocean basin that forms where one oceanic plate is forced underneath a continental plate or another oceanic plate (43)

P

pelagic (pi LAJ ik) **environment** the entire volume of water in the ocean and the marine organisms that live above the ocean floor; also known as the water environment (49)

permeability (PUHR mee uh BIL uh tee) a rock's ability to let water pass through it (14)

petroleum an oily mixture of flammable organic compounds from which liquid fossil fuels and other products are separated; crude oil (52)

plankton microscopic organisms that float at or near the ocean's surface (46)

point-source pollution pollution that comes from one particular source area (19)

porosity (poh RAHS uh tee) the amount of open space between individual rock particles (14)

precipitation solid or liquid water that falls from the air to the Earth (5, 39)

R

recharge zone the ground surface where water enters an aquifer (15)

renewable resource a natural resource that can be used and replaced over a relatively short time (22)

rift valley a valley that forms in a rift zone between diverging tectonic plates (43)

S

salinity a measure of the amount of dissolved salts and other solids in a given amount of liquid (36)

satellite a natural or artificial body that revolves around a planet (45)

scientific method a series of steps that scientists use to answer questions and solve problems (112)

seamount an individual mountain of volcanic material on the abyssal plain (43)

septic tank a large, underground tank that collects and cleans waste water from a household (21)

sewage treatment plant a factory that cleans waste materials out of water that comes from sewers or drains (20)

soil a loose mixture of small mineral fragments and organic material (11)

spring tides tides with maximum daily tidal range that occur during the new and full moons (86)

storm surge a local rise in sea level near the shore that is caused by strong winds from a storm, such as a hurricane (83)

surf the area between the breaker zone and the shore (80)

surface current a streamlike movement of water that occurs at or near the surface of the ocean (71, 73)

swells rolling waves that move in a steady procession across the ocean (81)

GLOSSARY

Glossary **129**

T

temperature a measure of how hot (or cold) something is (110)

thermocline a layer of ocean water extending from 300 m below sea level to about 700 m below sea level in which water temperature drops with increased depth faster than it does in other zones of the ocean (37)

tidal bore a body of water that rushes up through a narrow bay, estuary, or river channel during the rise of high tide, causing a very sudden tidal rise (87)

tidal range the difference between levels of ocean water at high tide and low tide (86)

tides daily movements of ocean water that change the level of the ocean's surface (84)

tributary a smaller stream or river that flows into a larger one (6)

trough (trahf) the lowest point of a wave (78)

tsunami a wave that forms when a large volume of ocean water is suddenly moved up or down (82)

U

upwelling a process in which cold, nutrient-rich water from the deep ocean rises to the surface and replaces warm surface water (77)

V

volume the amount of space that something occupies or the amount of space that something contains (121)

W

water cycle the continuous movement of water from water sources into the air, onto land, into and over the ground, and back to the water sources; a cycle that links all of the Earth's solid, liquid, and gaseous water together (4, 39)

watershed the land drained by a river system, which includes the main river and all of its tributaries (6)

water table an underground boundary where the zone of aeration and the zone of saturation meet (14)

wave height the vertical distance between a wave's crest and its trough (78)

wavelength the distance between two adjacent wave crests or wave troughs (78)

wave period the time between the passage of two wave crests (or troughs) at a fixed point (79)

whitecap a white, foaming wave with a very steep crest that breaks in the open ocean before the wave gets close to the shore (81)

Index

A **boldface** number refers to an illustration on that page.

A

abyssal plain, 42, **42**
abyssal zone, 48, **48**
acceleration, average, 125
Adopt-a-Beach program, 59, **59**
aeration zone, 14, **14**
agriculture, water usage in, 23
algal blooms, 95, **95**
alluvial fans, 13, **13**
alluvium, 11–13
Alvin (minisub), 41, **41**
Amazon River basin, 6
anglerfish, **49**
anhydrite, 126
aqualung, 66
aquifers, 14–15, **15**, 16, **16**, 23, **23**.
        See also ground water
aragonite, 126
Arctic Ocean, **34**
area
        calculation of, 121
        defined, 121
artesian springs, 16, **16**
Atlantic Ocean, **34**
averages, defined, 118

B

basin, deep-ocean, 42
bathyal zone, 48, **48**
bathymetric profile, **44**
bats, 17
Bay of Fundy (Canada), **87**
bed loads, **8**
benthic environment, 47
benthos, **46**, 47, **47**
beryl, 126
black smokers, 48
breakers, 80, **80**

C

calcite, 126
calcium carbonate, 17
California Current, **76**
Calypso II, 66, **66**
Canyonlands National Park (Utah),
        10
cap rocks, 16, **16**
carbonate minerals, 126
careers in science
        seismologist, 94

Carlsbad Caverns (New Mexico), **17**
caves, **17**, 17–18
Celsius scale, 110
channels, 7
chlorine, 36
chlorite, 126
clams, **48**
Clean Water Act of 1972, 58
cleavage, 127
climate
        oceans and, 40, **40**
        surface currents and, **76**, 76–77
color (of minerals), 126
concentration, calculation of, 125
concept mapping, 108
condensation, **5, 39**
conservation of energy
        law of, 124
continental deflections, 72, **72**
Continental Divide, 6, **6**
continental margin, 42, **42**
continental rise, **42**
continental shelf, **42**
continental slope, **42**
controlled experiments, 113
conversion tables, SI, 109
Cook Inlet (Alaska), 54
copper, 126
coral, 47, **47**
Coriolis effect, 72, **72**
Cousteau, Jacques, 66
crest, 78, **78**
currents
        climate and, 76, **76**
        deep, **74**, 74–75, **75**
        longshore, 81, **81**
        ocean, 70–77
        surface, **71**, 71–73, **72, 73**

D

Davis, William Morris, 9
decimals, 119
deep currents, 74–75, **74–75**
Deep Flight (minisub), 41, **41**
deep-ocean basin, 42–43, **42–43**
deltas, 12, 31
density
        calculation of, 125
        of ocean currents, 74, **74**
deposition
        in caves, 17
        by streams and rivers, 11–13,
        12, 13
desalination, 53
diamonds, 126
Dillo Dirt, 56
discharge, stream, 7
disease, 20
dissolved loads, **8**

dissolved solids, 36, **36, 74**. *See also* salt
divides, 6
dolphins, **49**
drainage basins, 6
drift nets, 50, **50**
drilling for oil, 52
dripstone, 17, **17**

E

Earth
        tides and, 84–87, **85, 86**
earthquakes
        tsunamis and, **82**, 82–83, 94
ecosystems
        threats to, 31
electricity
        from tidal energy, 54, **54**
El Niño, 77, **77**
energy
        tidal, 54, **54**
        wave, 54
Environmental Protection Agency
        (EPA), 55
erosion
        in caves, 17
        shoreline, 81
        streams and rivers, 4, **4**, 7–10, **8**
evaporation, **5**, 36, **39, 74**
experiments, controlled, 113
Exxon Valdez spill, 57

F

Fahrenheit–Celsius conversion,
        110
Fahrenheit scale, 110, **110**
first law of motion (Newton's),
        124
fish farming, 51, **51**
fishing, 50, **50**
flood plains, 10, 13, **13**
flow of water
        deposits from, 11–13, **12, 13**
        ground water, **14–16**, 14–18
        river systems, 6–10
        streams, 6–10
fluorite, 126
force(s)
        calculation of, 125
fractions, 119–120
fracture, 127
fresh water, 67
freshwater supply, 53
Fundy, Bay of, **87**

Credits

Abbreviations used: (t) top, (c) center, (b) bottom, (l) left, (r) right, (bkgd) background

ILLUSTRATIONS

All work, unless otherwise noted, contributed by Holt, Rinehart & Winston.

Chapter One: Page 5, Mike Wepplo/Das Group; 6(bc), MapQuest.com; 8, Uhl Studios, Inc.; 11(b), Marty Roper/Planet Rep; 14(cl), Stephen Durke/Washington Artists; 15(c), MapQuest.com; 15(br), Geoff Smith/Scott Hull; 16, Stephen Durke/Washington Artists; 20(b), John Huxtable/Black Creative; 21(cl), John Huxtable/Black Creative; 21(b), Sidney Jablonski; 23(c), MapQuest.com; 26(c), Mike Wepplo/Das Group; 29(cr), Sidney Jablonski.

Chapter Two: Page 35, MapQuest.com; 36(tl), Ross, Culbert and Lavery; 37(tr), MapQuest.com; 37(b), Ross, Culbert and Lavery; 39(b), Mike Wepplo/Das Group; 42–43(b), Uhl Studios, Inc.; 44(b), Uhl Studios, Inc.; 45(br), Ross, Culbert and Lavery; 46, Yuan Lee; 54(tl), Jared Schneidman Design; 57(br), Mark Heine; 63(c), Jared Schneidman Design; 64(c), Bill Mayer; 64(tr), MapQuest.com; 65(tr), Ross, Culbert and Lavery.

Chapter Three: Page 70(tr), Dean Fleming; 71(tr), Stephen Durke/Washington Artists; 71(bl), MapQuest.com; 72, MapQuest.com; 73(c), MapQuest.com; 74, Stephen Durke/Washington Artists; 75, Jared Schneidman Design; 76, MapQuest.com; 78, Jared Schneidman Design; 79, Jared Schneidman Design; 80, Dean Fleming; 82(c), Uhl Studios, Inc.; 83(t), MapQuest.com; 84(c), Marty Roper/Planet Rep; 85, Sidney Jablonski; 86, Sidney Jablonski; 90(br), Dean Fleming; 90(c), Stephen Durke/Washington Artists; 91(c), Marty Roper/Planet Rep; 93(cr), Sidney Jablonski

LabBook: Page 101(tr), Mark Heine; 105(br), Geoff Smith/Scott Hull; 106(b), Mark Heine; 107(b).

Appendix: Page 110(c), Terry Guyer; 114(b), Mark Mille/Sharon Langley; 122, Kristy Sprott; 123, Kristy Sprott.

PHOTOGRAPHY

Cover and Title Page: Yabb Arthus-Bertrand/Corbis

Sam Dudgeon/HRW Photo: p. viii-1, 22(bl), 52, 60(bl), 71, 78, 96(bl), 97(bc), 98(tr, br), 99(tl), 104, 111(br).

Table of Contents: v(tr), Laurence Parent; v(cr), Laurence B. Aiuppy/FPG International; v(b), Victoria Smith/HRW Photo; vi(tl), Rosentiel School of Marine & Atmospheric Sciences, University of Miami; vi(bl), Wayne Lynch/DRK Photo; vii(tr), Mike Bacon/Tom Stack & Associates; vii(b), Norbert Wu.

Chapter One: pp. 2-3 Frans Lanting/Minden Pictures; 3 HRW Photo; 4 Tom Bean/DRK Photo; 7(br), Ed Reschke/Peter Arnold, Inc.; 7(bl), Jim Work/Peter Arnold, Inc.; 9(br), Frans Lanting/Minden Pictures; 9(tr), Laurence Parent; 10(tl), The G.R. "Dick" Roberts Photo Library; 10(cl), Galen Rowell/Peter Arnold, Inc.; 12(tl), The Huntington Library/SuperStock; 12(cr), Earth Satellite Corporation/Science Photo Library/Photo Researchers, Inc.; 13(tr), Visuals Unlimited/Martin G. Miller; 13(cr), Earth Satellite Corporation; 17 Rich Reid/Animals Animals/Earth Scenes; 18 Leif Skoogfers/Woodfin Camp & Associates; 19(bl), Laurence B. Aiuppy/FPG International; 19(tr), Wayne Lynch/DRK Photo; 22(tl), Arthus Bertrand/ Explorer/Photo Researchers, Inc.; 24 Victoria Smith/HRW Photo; 27(c), Rich Reid/Animals Animals/Earth Scenes; 28(bl), Donald Nausbaum/Stone; 28(tr), TSA/Tom Stack & Associates; 30 Jeff and Alexa Henry; 31 C.C. Lockwood/DRK Photo.

Chapter Two: pp. 32-33 Stuart Westmorland/Photo Researchers, Inc.; 33 HRW Photo; 34 Tom Van Sant, Geosphere Project/Planetary Visions/Science Photo Library; 38 U.S. Navy; 40(cl), Rosentiel School of Marine and Atmospheric Science, University of Miami; 41(br), James Wilson/Woodfin Camp & Associates; 41(bl), Norbert Wu; 45 NOAA/NSDS; 47(br), Mike Bacon/Tom Stack & Associates; 47(cr), Jim Zipp/Photo Researchers, Inc.; 48(tl), James B. Wood; 48(cl), Al Glddings/Al Giddings Images; 48(bl), JAMESTEC; 49(tr), E. R. Degginger/Color-Pic, Inc.; 49(cr), Nobert Wu; 50 Paolo Curto/UP/Bruce Coleman, Inc.; 51(br), Bryan and Cherry Alexander Photography; 51(cl), Breg Vaughn/Tom Stack & Associates; 52(cr), TGS-NOPEC Geophysical Company; 53(bl), Institute of Oceanographic Sciences/NERC/Science Photo Library/Photo Researchers, Inc.; 53(bc), Charles D. Winters/Photo Researchers, Inc.; 55(b), E. R. Degginger/Color-Pic, Inc.; 56(cl), Photo Edit; 56(bc), Andy Christiansen/HRW Photo; 56(br), Ron Chapple/FPG International; 57(tr), Ben Osborne/Stone; 57(bl), Courtesy Mobil; 58 Andy Christiansen/HRW Photo; 59(tl, tr), Courtesy Texas General Land Office Adopt-A-Beach Program; 62 James Wilson/Woodfin Camp & Associates; 66 Gilles Bassignac/Liaison Agency; 67 SuperStock.

Chapter Three: pp. 68-69 O. Brown, R Evans, and M. Carle, University of Miami Rosenstiel School of Marine and Atmospheric Science, Miami, Florida; 69 HRW Photo; 70(cr), Hulton Getty/Liaison Agency; 77 Lacy Atkins/San Francisco Examiner/AP/Wide World Photos; 81(tr), CC Lockwood/Bruce Coleman, Inc.; 81(bl), Darrell Wong/Stone; 81(br), August Upitis/FPG International; 82 Denis J. Sigrist, International Tsunami Center, Honolulu, HI/National Geophysical Data; 87(tl, tr), VOSCAR/The Maine Photographer; 88 Andy Christiansen/HRW Photo; 91(cl), Art Resource, NY; 92(tl), Warren Bolster/ Stone; 92(br), Fred Whitehead/Animals Animals/Earth Scenes; 94(tl), Todd Bigelow/HRW Photo; 94(br), Warren Bolster/Stone; 95(tc), J.A.L. Cooke/Oxford Scientific Films/Animals Animals/Earth Scenes; 95(tr), Visuals Unlimited/ David M. Williams.

LabBook/Appendix: "LabBook Header", "L", Corbis Images; "a", Letraset Phototone; "b", and "B", HRW; "o", and "k", images ©2001 PhotoDisc/HRW; 97(tr), John Langford/HRW Photo; 97(cl), Michelle Bridwell/HRW Photo; 97(br), Image ©2001 PhotoDisc, Inc./HRW; 98(bl), Stephanie Morris/HRW Photo; 98(cl), Victoria Smith/HRW Photo; 99(b) Peter Van Steen; 99(tr), Jana Birchum/HRW Photo; 102 Victoria Smith/HRW Photo; 103 Andy Christiansen/HRW Photo; 107 Victoria Smith/HRW Photo; 111(tr), Peter Van Steen/HRW Photo.

Feature Borders: Unless otherwise noted below, all images copyright ©2001 PhotoDisc/HRW. "Across the Sciences" 66, all images by HRW; "Careers" 94, sand bkgd and Saturn, Corbis Images; DNA, Morgan Cain & Associates; scuba gear, ©1997 Radlund & Associates for Artville; "Eye on the Environment" 31, 67, clouds and sea in bkgd, HRW; bkgd grass, red eyed frog, Corbis Images; hawks, pelican, Animals Animals/Earth Scenes; rat, Visuals Unlimited/John Grelach; endangered flower, Dan Suzio/Photo Researchers, Inc.; "Health Watch" 95, dumbbell, Sam Dudgeon/HRW Photo; aloe vera, EKG, Victoria Smith/HRW Photo; basketball, ©1997 Radlund & Associates for Artville; shoes, bubbles, Greg Geisler; "Weird Science" 30, mite, David Burder/Stone; atom balls, J/B Woolsey Associates; walking stick, turtle, EclectiCollection.

Self-Check Answers

Chapter 1—The Flow of Fresh Water

Page 8: If a river slowed down, the suspended load would be deposited.

Page 12: Answers will vary. A river might slow where there is a bend, where the gradient decreases, or where the river empties into a large body of water.

Page 16: The impermeable rock layer in the aquifer traps the water in the permeable layer below. This creates the pressure needed to form an artesian spring.

Chapter 2—Exploring the Oceans

Page 35: If North America and South America continue to drift westward and Asia continues to drift eastward, the continents will eventually collide on the other side of the Earth.

Page 43: Rift valleys form where tectonic plates pull apart, and ocean trenches form where one oceanic plate is forced underneath a continental plate or another oceanic plate.

Chapter 3—The Movement of Ocean Water

Page 71: Because he was traveling from Peru to a Polynesian island to the west, Heyerdahl would have noticed the wind blowing from the east.